Join the Club
Idioms for Academic and Social Success

Lisa Naylor

McGraw-Hill
Contemporary

McGraw-Hill/Contemporary

A Division of The McGraw-Hill Companies

Join the Club 2, 1st Edition

Printed in the United States of America.

1 2 3 4 5 6 7 8 9 10   VH   07 06 05 04 03 02 01

ISBN: 0-07-242804-X
ISBN: 0-07-112387-3 (ISE)

Editorial Director: *Tina B. Carver*
Developmental Editor: *Louis Carrillo*
Director of Marketing: *Thomas P. Dare*
Production Manager: *Genevieve Kelley*
Interior Designer: *Michael Warrell, Design Solutions*
Compositor: *Tracey Harris*
Typeface: *10/13 Palatino*
Printer: *Von Hoffman Graphics*

INTERNATIONAL EDITION ISBN 0-07-112387-3

TABLE OF CONTENTS

CHAPTER   PAGE

1 catch on, a break, the whole nine yards, push one's luck, straight,   1
wine and dine, buy something, guts, cut out for, funky,
make out, yuppie, jazzed, in a nutshell, ask for it

2 a tip, spaced out, have what it takes, schmooze, food for thought,   19
a fake, get even, deal with, cut corners, speak of the devil,
a wimp, keep up on, get away with, grow on someone, bend over backwards

3 play it by ear, a rain check, uptight, off the hook, go out on,   39
off the wall, tailgate, bring up, bite off more than you can chew, wisecracks,
set up, a drag, the ball's in your court, on the level, burned out

4 the bottom line, tacky, hold out, twist my arm, click,   57
a hassle, off base, snooze, max out, hit it off,
glitch, savvy, pick up, can't be beat, flip out

5 a klutz, phony, come up with, right up your alley, know the ropes,   75
a rookie, picky, glued to, spin your wheels, cold turkey,
red tape, sleazy, chip in, stick your neck out, grin and bear it

6 count on, through the grapevine, decent, give it a shot, a hunch,   93
on someone's case, knock on wood, call off, play hardball, glutton
for punishment, a tough act to follow, fall back on, come out smelling
like a rose, lighten up, crooked

7 burn your bridges, touchy, practical joke, pull something off, a taste   111
of your own medicine, the runaround, bail someone out, pumped up,
draw the line, cranky, catch off guard, wiped out, a one-track mind,
carry weight, gripe

8 slick, the back burner, chew out, a comeback, get up the nerve,   131
below the belt, move on, lame, an ivory tower, make ends meet,
bounce ideas off someone, wacky, a geek, add up, ahead of the game

CHAPTER REVIEWS

APPENDICES

TO THE TEACHER

Level 2

Join the Club: Idioms for Academic and Social Success was written for low-intermediate to advanced nonnative speakers of English. Level 2 is intended for high-intermediate to advanced levels. Each level was written with a two-part objective. The first part is to introduce students to the most frequently occurring idiomatic expressions; in other words, the colloquial speech actually heard outside the classroom. Because of the frequency of expressions, included in some chapters are slang expressions that have been selected for their saliency and "safeness," such as **bail someone out** or **decent**.

The second part of the objective is to foster communicative competence through engaging students in integrated skills tasks. Not only do students practice the expressions through listening, speaking, reading and writing activities, but they are also given opportunities to discuss and reflect on the sociolinguistic features generally associated with the expressions. This helps to raise register awareness of the language: who uses the expressions (young, old, male, female, etc.), in which types of situations the expressions are used (at school, at work, among friends, etc.), and how the expressions are used (happy, sad, sarcastic, neutral, etc.). For example, **twist my arm** is an expression that is usually used among friends or acquaintances and may be said in a friendly tone of voice. However, if **you bite off more than you can chew**, you may be complaining about something you have to do at school or work. Students greatly appreciate being exposed to such meaningful and useful information about their second language and the society in which it is spoken. This not only helps them to communicate more naturally with native speakers through using such high-frequency expressions but also to develop an awareness of sociocultural expectations as well as to discriminate among individuals they may encounter in their second-language environment.

Join the Club was designed to access all learner styles and to be student-centered. The activities in the book revolve around students working together to maximize cooperative learning. However, most of the activities are also suitable for the individual student who prefers to work alone. Suggestions for grouping students are provided, although effective student grouping is ultimately left to the discretion of the instructor. Many students naturally self-group as they progress through the chapters. Because the book is student-centered, the teacher is free to circulate around the classroom and therefore give more individualized attention.

There are 120 target expressions presented explicitly in eight chapters, which consist of 15 expressions each. In addition to the target expressions, in Part III of each chapter there are expansions to the target expressions. For example, the target expression **grow on someone** is similar to **rub off on someone**. Further expansions include to **rub someone the wrong way** and to **get on someone's nerves**. Because of this feature in Part III of every chapter, there are over 200 more expressions explained, practiced and reviewed in **Join the Club 2.** There are also a number of expressions used in context. Every expression can be found in Appendix D, the Index/Glossary, which contains over 700 entries.

Each chapter follows a consistent five-part design to systematically introduce, practice, and apply the 15 target expressions and the expanded expressions. Due to the large number of expressions in each chapter, after every two chapters there is a review designed to provide further practice of all the expressions.

Each chapter begins with the 15 target expressions divided into groups of five, which represent a variety of grammatical categories: nouns, phrasal verbs, verbs, adjectives, and adverbs. Following are suggestions for use:

■ **Part I**

Work It Out—Grouping Strategy: Divide the students into groups 1, 2 and 3. For example, Student Group 1 studies the five expressions on pages 2–3. Student Group 2 studies the five expressions on pages 4–5. Student Group 3 studies the expressions on pages 6–7. Explain to the students that, in their group, they will study five new expressions and complete four exercises together. The four exercises are

1) **Quick Match**—match the expression to an abbreviated definition

2) **Cloze It**—read the sentence and fill in the blank with the appropriate expression while paying attention to grammar requirements.

3) **Sense or Nonsense**—discuss the sentences to decide if they do or don't make sense (i.e. It can be very satisfying to give someone a taste of their own medicine.)

4) **Plug In**—replace the underlined phrases with the appropriate expression while observing grammar requirements. (15-20 minutes)

■ **Part II**

Information Gap—This is the trickiest part of the book, but please note that after one chapter, most students understand the logic behind the design of the book.

Grouping Strategy: After each student group has studied 5 expressions, re-group the students so that all three groups are working together. Because the purpose of the **Information Gap** is to maximize meaning negotiation through listening to and verifying what each other said, the instructor must explain to the students that

• they will be introduced to the other 10 expressions of the chapter by testing their classmate who just studied them, and

• it is very important that they look at their assigned pages to fully benefit from this activity. For example, Student 1 will look at pages 2–3 while Student 2 and Student 3 ask the Information Gap questions on page 8. Student 1 must listen and explain to Students 2 and 3, who write down the answers as given.

The two **Information Gap** tasks are (1) **Tell Me**—students directly ask for the expression and write it down, and (2) **Make This Make Sense**—students have to figure out a way to make the sentences make sense, usually through changing one or two words. As the instructor circulates around the classroom, it's a great idea to encourage the students to look for more than one way to make the sentences make sense. This not only invites discussion among the students, but also reinforces grammar and vocabulary knowledge.

After the three rounds of the **Information Gap** are completed, tell the students they must complete all of Part I of the chapter. This may be assigned as an in-class assignment or for homework. Tell them to consult Appendix B—the Answer Key. (15—20 minutes)

■ **Part III**

It's Halftime—There are four Halftime Activities, which begin with the **Expression Guide**, the purpose of which is to initiate a discussion about register. With native speakers outside the class, or in-class as a whole class or small-group activity, students are encouraged to inquire about how, when, where, and by whom the expressions may be used. The instructor may wish to make an overhead of the **Expression Guide** on which to write any important sociolinguistic features that pertain to certain expressions. For example, the expression I **don't buy it** may be said with a suspicious tone of voice. Encourage the students to fill the **Expression Guide** up with any meaningful information about the expressions and share what they discover with each other.

The **Expression Guide** is also an ideal activity for the instructor to invite the students to compare expressions from their own cultures to those they are studying. The instructor may also wish to expand on some meanings of the expressions as they come up. For example, the slang item schmooze sometimes has a derogatory meaning. This could invite an interesting discussion. (10–30 minutes, depending on the class and the expressions).

The second activity in Part III is **Find Out**, a meaning/grammar expansion of selected expressions. Any expression that carries important grammatical information and/or further meaning uses is presented, explained, and followed up with a practice exercise. These expanded expressions are marked with one asterisk in the Index-Glossary.

After the students complete **Find Out**, they engage in a reading and discussion activity in which all of the target and expanded expressions are underlined and used in short stories. The students work in pairs or small groups and take turns reading aloud and explaining, in their own words, the meanings of the underlined expressions. This is also the activity in which more expressions are used in context. Because the students have already studied the target and expanded chapter expressions, they are able to guess and explain the meaning of many new expressions that haven't been explicitly presented. This is a highly engaging activity and very effective for building confidence. During this activity, the instructor can circulate around the classroom to listen to the students and discuss with them whatever the reading inspires them to think about. (15 minutes)

The final activity of **Part III** is the **Expression Log**. This is a two-part activity which should be completed out of class. The students ought to keep their **Expression Log** in a small notebook, which the instructor will collect to provide feedback to return to the students. In the first part of the activity, the students are asked to choose any 15 expressions from the chapter to use in original sentences or paragraphs to demonstrate that they understand the meaning of the expressions. The instructor may suggest that the students personalize their entries by being creative and even writing stories. This is excellent for memory retention. Students can share what they write with their classmates, which is a very enjoyable expansion to the first part of the **Expression Log**.

The second part of the **Expression Log** is to have the students record a minimum of two new expressions following the **New Expression Guide** in Appendix A. They can keep track of their expressions on the **New Expression List** also located in Appendix A. Because the **Expression Log** is a natural place to provide students with further individualized attention, the instructor should encourage the students to communicate any questions about the expressions they may have.

It is very is important to collect, correct, and return the **Expression Logs** to the students. It is also recommended to keep an on-going list of the new expressions the students bring to class. The instructor can select the most salient expressions brought to the class by the students, put them on a class list, and then have the students explain their expressions to each other. This also serves as an excellent review of all the expressions the students have studied because they have to look over their **Expression Log** entries to teach the expressions that they brought to class to each other.

■ Part IV

Tune In—Now that the students have learned the expressions, it is time to apply them. The **Tune In** listening tasks, of which there are 8 variations, are designed to make the students apply the expressions through either contextualized meaning expansion (i.e., listening for contextual clues which elicit the expression) or listening for meaning (i.e., did that make sense, was the expression used properly?). After each **Tune In**, be sure to allow time for student discussion. The transcripts for the **Tune In** tasks are in Appendix C. Before doing a **Tune In** listening task, be sure to read over the instructions with the students to make sure they understand. Allow time for them to look over the format and explain that each item will be repeated two or three times. (15 minutes)

■ Part V

The Chat Room—There are also eight variations to this final chapter activity, which is a conversational board game designed to maximize turn taking with a roll of the die and an optional minute timer. The instructor may want to use the minute timer for the group that has a combination of gregarious and reticent students. By circulating and listening to the students during **The Chat Room** activity, the instructor can also ascertain how well the students have learned the expressions of each chapter. If supplemental practice is needed, consult the Suggestion Box on pages xi. (20 minutes)

Reviews: After every two chapters, there is a review designed to practice the target 15 expressions as well as the expanded expressions from each chapter. For easy reference, all of the expressions (target, expanded, and contextualized) have been put on a list at the beginning of each review. The review activities include groupwork games such as tic-tac-toe, bingo, and Jeopardy and information gap activities such as one-sided dialogues, Password, and word puzzles. There are also activity competitions designed to see how well and fast the students can remember and produce the expressions while also considering the context.

General Notes
Pronunciation: Every activity in **Join the Club** has been designed to maximize cooperative learning by integrating the skills of listening, speaking, reading, and writing through building upon meaning negotiation, vocabulary expansion,

and grammar reinforcement. There are several ways to integrate pronunciation in every chapter. First of all, after the students have finished **Parts I** and **II**, the instructor can say each expression and read some of the exercises using the expressions. The students can repeat after the instructor, which also lets them review what they have just studied. The sentences in **Part III Read and Discuss** may also be used the same way. This traditional listen and repeat pronunciation exercise provides an opportunity to practice the important elements of contractions, reductions, and deletions in English pronunciation. It also provides useful intonation practice. This not only gives students a chance to be expressive but also helps them to recognize thought groups and focus words. If instructors choose to practice pronunciation in this manner, remember to be as animated as possible so that the students can hear these elements of pronunciation. Also, because **Join the Club** is a student-centered textbook, the instructor may choose to address pronunciation on an individualized basis while circulating around the classroom. Some final suggestions for practicing pronunciation is to have the students perform the **Dialogue Matches** from the **Reviews**, write and perform a role-play or chain story, and read aloud from their Expression Logs. These are great for reviewing expressions as well as for practicing pronunciation.

Selection of Expressions: Every expression in **Join the Club** has been carefully researched and selected for its saliency and high-frequency use. This was done over years of teaching idioms and slang both in the United States and overseas. All of the expressions come from students who read or heard them somewhere—in a class, at work, from a friend, while traveling, from a movie, a TV show, a song, the radio, the newspaper, a magazine, a novel, etc. I compiled a master list of all the expressions the students came up with, no matter how many times they occurred. For example, in one year alone, over 126 students heard **check it out**!

After choosing the most frequently occurring expressions, I consulted several specialized dictionaries for the purpose of building in the sociolinguistic aspect to **Join the Club**. I wanted to verify if the expressions were idioms, slang words, jargon, argot, colloquialisms, vernacularisms, proverbs, formal or informal language, etc. Because it is the nature of language to overlap in defining if a particular expression is, for example, an idiom or a colloquialism, for the purpose of **Join the Club**, I decided to simplify and label only the slang items.

Finally, the expressions in each chapter were purposely not chosen to fit into a particular theme. If a textbook is organized using a theme-based approach, expressions are selected for the sake of the theme rather than their saliency or frequency of use. If native speakers rarely use such expressions, why make students learn them? As previously mentioned, every expression in **Join the Club** was selected for its saliency and high-frequency occurrence, and the expressions for each chapter were chosen based on their grammatical category as well as their semantic features. In every chapter there is a variety of nouns, verbs, phrasal verbs, adjectives, and adverbs, all of which carry a variety of meaning associations: positive, negative, funny, serious, neutral, etc. The rationale behind this type of selection of expressions is based on first language acquisition theory: provide the learner with a rich variety of lexical items from which to choose to create and embed meaning. I'm confident that when your students write their **Expression Logs**, that when you listen to them engage in meaning negotiation activities, such as **Sense or Nonsense**, **Make this Make Sense**, and **The Chat Room**, you will be very pleased with the results!

A Special Note For English-as-a-Foreign-Language Instructors: Whether you are a native speaker or a non-native speaker, one of the biggest challenges in teaching EFL is not only finding authentic material to use in the classroom, but also finding native speakers or fluent speakers with whom your student can practice. In Part III of every chapter, I suggest making the **Expression Guide** a whole class or small group activity. For students to complete the second part of the **Expression Log**, both you and your students can bring into the classroom whatever is available in English on the radio, in music, on television, at the movies, in an English language newspaper, magazine or book, on the Internet, and so on.

—LN

SUGGESTION BOX

More Ways to Practice Using the Expressions

GAMES

1. **Tic-Tac-Toe:** Create your own game.

2. **Bingo:** Make a grid of 25 squares. Choose 25 expressions and ask your classmates to write them in the grid. Then describe the expressions. The first person to get 5 in a row is the winner.

3. **Password:** On index cards, write expressions of your choice to practice describing to your partner.

4. **Hot Seat:** In groups of 3 or 4, one person is seated on the "hot seat" and cannot see the board. The teacher writes an expression on the board for the students to describe to the person on the hot seat. As soon as the person knows the expression, he or she jumps up and shouts it out. The first group to get the expression wins a point.

5. **Hangman:** Practice spelling by playing this game.

6. **The Great Race:** Students form teams of 4 or 5. One student, or the teacher, randomly chooses expressions to describe. Whichever team writes the expression on the board the fastest wins.

7. **Jeopardy:** Arrange the expressions into categories. For example: Expressions that have two meanings: go out on, off base, make out, etc., Expressions with the word red: red tape, roll out the red carpet, in the red, etc., Expressions which may be said in an annoyed tone: uptight, a klutz, cranky, etc.

   Cover the target expressions or hints on the grid with adhesive notes. Select students to be the game host and contestants. A student contestant may say, "I'll try red for 5 points." The student host will say, "What is an expression that means to be in debt?" (Answer: in the red), etc.

8. **Mime:** Select expressions which lend themselves to being mimed: talk someone's ears off, be beat, crack up, down-to-earth, a backseat driver...

9. **Whispers:** One student writes a sentence using target expressions and then whispers it to the next student who repeats it around the room until the final student hears it.

10. **Basketball:** Divide the class into two teams. Select 3 point expressions and 2 point expressions. Fouls are given for wrong definitions, inability to define, speaking out of turn. Free throws are given for any foul.

11. **Baseball:** On the board, draw a baseball diamond and use adhesive notes with team names on them. Select expressions for single, double, and home-run questions. Each team member gets one chance to define the expression or spell it correctly. Any error is a strike. Three strikes and you're out.

12. **Big Bucks Pyramid:** On index cards, write expressions which have synonyms or antonyms. Put the cards face down. One student selects the card and reads the expression to the other student, who must come up with either a synonym or antonym. Encourage the students to go as fast as possible. Whichever team gets through the most cards goes to the top of the pyramid.

13. **Go Fish:** In pairs, students draw one expression, write a two-line dialogue within 2 minutes, and perform it for the class.

14. **Chain Story:** One student begins a story using a target expression in a sentence. The next student continues the story by writing another sentence and so on. The group of students who writes a story using the greatest number of expressions wins.

15. **List It:** In a limited time, students write down as many expressions as they can remember.

EXPRESSION LOGS

Students should be invited to share their Expression Logs with each other. The instructor can compile a selection of examples while leaving out the students' names. Students can then read what their classmates have written and enjoy guessing who wrote what. This is also a great way to indirectly practice pronunciation.

NEW EXPRESSIONS: CHAPTER CREATION

As a mid or final project, put the students into groups of 2 or 3 to create their own **Join the Club** chapter using some of the expressions they have brought to class in their Expression Logs. The students can model their chapter after those in the book. The teacher can also require that certain components be included in the chapters that the students create. For example:

> Definitions and Examples, Quick Fix, Cloze It, Sense or Nonsense, Make this Make Sense, Tune In, or The Chat Room.

Students can share their chapters with their classmates. They can also make a textbook of all their chapters.

BINGO

		BINGO		

JEOPARDY—Use adhesive notes to cover the boxes with the target expressions or hints.

POINTS	Expressions that	Expressions that	Expressions that	Expressions that
5				
10				
15				
20				

TO THE STUDENT

Welcome to **Join the Club!** Every language has many idioms and slang expressions, but did you know that English has more expressions than any other language? There are over 600,000 words in English, most of which are borrowed from other languages. This makes the English language highly idiomatic. How on earth can you learn so many expressions?

I wrote this book to introduce you to the most frequently and commonly used idiomatic and slang expressions. The expressions in **Join the Club** were selected with this goal in mind: to present you, the students, with the most up-to-date (**yuppies**), popular (**figure out**), and here-to-stay expressions (**knock on wood**). Because the expressions in this book are so common, you may have heard many of them already. But do you know what they mean? Do you know how to use them?

There are three goals of **Join the Club**. You will:

1) learn the expressions by understanding the meaning(s) and nuances such as formal, informal, friendly, excited, upset, and sarcastic.

2) practice using the expressions by completing exercises in class with your classmates and out of class with native speakers or wherever you can find some English, and

3) look for more expressions outside the classroom on your own by keeping your own Expression Log, which is a notebook of your own personal practice.

Every chapter in **Join the Club** has five parts. It is better to work with your classmates to complete most of the parts, but you can also work alone. To learn and practice the expressions so that you can remember them, you will do listening, speaking, reading, and writing exercises and play games. You will also practice grammar and use a lot of vocabulary to learn the expressions. To fully benefit, you should complete all the activities in every chapter. That way you'll be able to remember the expressions to use them when you want to.

You can check your answers in the Answer Key in Appendix B. Pay attention to the grammar points as well! If you have questions about the meaning or grammar of some expressions, you can look in the Index/Glossary in Appendix D.

Be sure to ask your teacher, friends, and acquaintances any questions you may have.

—LN

ACKNOWLEDGEMENTS

A huge thank you goes to the University of California, San Diego English Language Programs for attracting all the international students who have taken my idioms and slang classes over the years. A very special thank you to the Director, Mr. Peter Thomas, and the Assistant Director, Ms. Roxanne Nuhaily, for their support and enthusiasm for **Join the Club**.

I'd also like to thank the people at McGraw-Hill for their effort in getting **Join the Club** published. Finally, I'd like to thank my husband, Carlos, for all of his support and encouragement. This book is for him.

—LN

C H A P T E R

1

wine and dine

catch on

a break

the whole nine yards

push one's luck

straight

buy something

guts

be cut out for

funky

make out

yuppie

jazzed

in a nutshell

ask for it

Work It Out

Student Group 1

Learn the meanings of the following five expressions by completing the exercises. Work with Student Group 1 or by yourself.

■ **GUESS** the meanings of the five expressions.

1) Liz is sharp! She just started working here, but she's catching on fast.

2) Michael got his break into professional comedy after he met Adam Sandler, a Hollywood superstar.

3) What a fun party—great food, music, and people! Carlos really went the whole nine yards!

4) I know you're beating the odds right now, but you're pushing your luck if you keep on playing.

5) The Smiths are pretty straight people, so be careful what you say.

■ **CHECK OUT** the definitions and examples of the expressions.

1) catch on—understand how to do something, usually slowly, but often quickly; become popular or trendy.
   Techno music caught on even more after Madonna's "Ray of Light" album came out.

2) a break—lucky chance or opportunity; be lenient, go easy on someone.
   The teacher gave me a break and let me turn in my homework late.

3) the whole nine yards—to do or get everything, go all out.
   Wow— roses, chocolate, dinner and dancing. He went the whole nine yards.

4) push one's luck—continue to risk something after initial success.
   You were late for class and now you want to leave early? Don't push your luck!

5) straight—traditional, conservative; speak frankly, directly.
   Look, I have to be straight with you. I think you have a drinking problem.

■ **QUICK FIX**—Match the expressions to the words that are similar.

1) everything under the sun   _____a break

2) keep going for it   _____catch on

3) conventional   _____ the whole nine yards

4) a fortunate event   _____ push your luck

5) comprehend   _____ straight

■ **CLOZE IT**—Use one of the above expressions to complete the sentences. Be sure to pay attention to any necessary grammatical changes.

1) Bruce got _____ when he played piano in a bar and everyone loved him.

2) New skis and boots AND a ski pass! Wow—_____.

3) You did all that already? Wow—you_____quickly!

4) Honesty is the best policy. Just be_____.

5) Don't _____with me and ask for more money. What have you done with all the money I've already given you anyway?

■ **SENSE OR NONSENSE**—With your classmates, discuss the sentences and decide if they do or don't make sense.

1) Because of all the scandals, the President really pushed his luck with the public._____

2) Some people get more breaks than others._____

3) Most politicians are straight about how they get campaign funds._____

4) They had a shotgun wedding at a drive through church in Las Vegas—the whole nine yards._____

5) Einstein caught on to physics when he was just a teenager._____

■ **PLUG IT IN**—Use the expressions to replace the underlined words. Make sure to check your grammar. Check the Index/Glossary for words you may not know.

1) They don't like any protests because they are pretty <u>conservative</u> politically.

2) Ozlem made a tough decision, but she got <u>the opportunity</u> she deserved.

3) Scott kept <u>taking advantage of his girlfriend</u>, but he finally got dumped.

4) Shigeko <u>figured out</u> her job so fast that she already got a raise.

5) When I get a new car, I want <u>the works: everything fully loaded</u>.

Student Group 2

Learn the meanings of the following five expressions by completing the exercises. Work with Student Group 2 or by yourself.

■ **GUESS** the meanings of the five expressions.

1) We have to **wine and dine** our potential clients to get their business.

2) There is no way Olivier paid cash for that BMW himself even though he says he did. I **don't buy it!**

3) It takes **guts** to face the truth sometimes.

4) Doug wasn't **cut out for** being a surgeon. He couldn't stand the sight of blood.

5) I love your pants—they're totally **funky!** Did you get them at that beach boutique?

■ **CHECK OUT** the definitions and examples of the expressions.

1) **wine and dine**—treat someone to something nice, usually a meal, although usually with an ulterior motive, business or personal.
Romeo wined and dined Juliet at Chez Lautrec.

2) **buy something**—believe or accept something, usually used in the negative.
My teacher didn't buy my story about leaving my homework in the Grand Canyon.

3) **guts**—courage, strength, or the nerve to do something.
Bill Gates has a lot of guts to take on the entire computer industry.

4) **be cut out for**—be suitable for or capable of doing something.
Ricky Martin is definitely cut out for superstardom.

5) **funky**—*interesting and stylish in an unconventional or exotic way.*
Pulp Fiction *is one of the funkiest movies I have ever seen.*

■ **QUICK FIX**—Match the expressions to the words that are similar.

1) able to do   _____ guts

2) flatter   _____ buy it

3) bravery   _____ wine and dine

4) believe   _____ funky

5) unique   _____ be cut out for

■ **CLOZE IT**—Use one of the above expressions to complete the sentences. Be sure to pay attention to any necessary grammatical changes.

1) I enjoy letting my boyfriend _____ me!

2) Michael Jordan _____ basketball, but not for baseball!

3) It took _____, but Chris asked for a promotion and he got it!

4) We had a very _____ vacation in Baja California, so full of adventure!

5) Gina _____ a word her boyfriend says because he has lied so much in the past.

■ **SENSE OR NONSENSE**—With your classmates, discuss the sentences and decide if they do or don't make sense.

1) Super straight people usually love to watch funky movies._____

2) It's easy to buy what a two-timer says._____

3) Wining and dining business clients sometimes works._____

4) Pro football players need to have a lot of guts._____

5) Graduates from top law schools such as Harvard University aren't cut out for being defense attorneys._____

■ **PLUG IT IN**—Use the expressions to replace the underlined words. Make sure to check your grammar. Check the Index/Glossary for words you may not know.

1) Henry Ford was definitely <u>made for</u> doing business.

2) It takes a lot of <u>spirit</u> to live in another country for a long time.

3) They really <u>rolled out the red carpet for</u> us last night! We had an amazing time.

4) I just <u>don't believe</u> my stockbroker's tip even though he is usually right!

5) San Francisco is one of the <u>most original</u> cities in the United States.

Student Group 3

Learn the meanings of the following five expressions by completing the exercises. Work with Student Group 3 or by yourself.

■ **GUESS** the meanings of the five expressions.

1) If we stick to the schedule, we'll **make out** fine.

2) Ever since Frank won his first few cases, he has turned into **a yuppie**, cruising around Beverly Hills in his Porsche.

3) Shin got 600 on the TOEFL. I bet he's totally **jazzed**!

4) There's not too much to tell you. **In a nutshell**, we lost the game. That's it!

5) I swear, if you interrupt me again, you're **asking for it**!

■ **CHECK OUT** the definitions and examples of the expressions.

1) make out—do well, be OK, succeed.
   Dorothy made out very well when she sold her stock as soon as it doubled.

2) yuppie—"young urban professional"—a young adult with a decent job who is materialistic and cares about following the latest trends of the "in" crowd.
   Janice used to be down-to-earth, but since she inherited all that money she has become a yuppie.

3) jazzed—very pleased, happy, thrilled, excited, stoked!
   I have enough frequent flyer miles to fly anywhere in the world FREE! I'm jazzed!

4) in a nutshell—describe something without going into too much detail; summarize
   "How was your date Saturday night?"
   "In a nutshell, I got home by 10:00!"

5) ask for it—look for trouble, make something (usually) bad happen.
   If you're late again, you'll be asking for it!

■ **QUICK FIX**—Match the expressions to the words that are similar.

1) often superficial   _____jazzed

2) invite problems   _____yuppie

3) briefly   _____make out

4) elated   _____in a nutshell

5) fare well   _____ask for it

■ **CLOZE IT**—Use one of the above expressions to complete the sentences. Be sure to pay attention to any necessary grammatical changes.

1) You must _____ about your trip to Brazil! When are you leaving?

2) We _____ like bandits at that sale! Look at how much we got for how little we spent!

3) There are a lot of _____ in the overpriced and trendy Marina District of San Francisco.

4) There were a lot of computer glitches but _____ everything went fine.

5) You'd better get new tires or you _____!

■ **SENSE OR NONSENSE**—With your classmates, discuss the sentences and decide if they do or don't make sense.

1) Gary is such a yuppie. That's why he still drives that old truck of his._____

2) I know you're in a hurry, so I'll explain everything to you in a nutshell._____

3) If Bill, who is married, continues to see Mary, who is single, he'll be asking for it!_____

4) The Asian economy made out very well in 1998._____

5) Most people are jazzed the day they get married._____

■ **PLUG IT IN**—Use the expressions to replace the underlined words. Make sure to check your grammar. Check the Index/Glossary for words you may not know.

1) How did you <u>do</u> at your job interview? Do you think they'll hire you?

2) Hey bro—check out the waves, man! They're rolling in. I'm totally <u>stoked</u>!

3) <u>To make a long story short</u>, we ended up leaving at 3:00 a.m.

4) Tracy cares too much about appearances because she's <u>slightly shallow</u>.

5) You're <u>going to be in hot water</u> if you keep sleeping in class.

Questions to Ask Someone from Student Group 1

Ask Student 1 the following questions. He or she will tell you the answers. You should write down the answers. Student 1 can look at pages 2-3 to find the answers.

■ **TELL ME:** Ask Student 1 the following questions to get the expressions.

1) How can you describe someone with a fairly conventional outlook?_____

2) Is there an expression that means to keep risking it?_____

3) What is a way to say you want it all?_____

4) What do you say when you want someone to go easy on you?_____

5) How can you explain that something has become a fad?_____

■ **MAKE THIS MAKE SENSE:** Ask Student 1 to change these sentences to make sense.

1) Really straight people love to go to the horse races and push their luck betting on the horses.

2) It was no problem at all getting a straight answer out of Rick, from the used car dealership, about the bottomline price of the 1991 Toyota.

3) My husband gave me the whole nine yards for our twenty-fifth anniversary: a gift certificate for a discount store!

4) American football has really caught on big time in Brazil.

5) I was going over 100 m.p.h. in a 35 m.p.h. zone, but the cop gave me a break and said, "See you in court!"

Questions to Ask Someone from Student Group 2

Ask Student 2 the following questions. He or she will tell you the answers. You should write down the answers. Student 2 can look at pages 4-5 to find the answers.

■ **TELL ME:** Ask Student 2 the following questions to get the expressions.

1) How do you say you are suspicious of something?_____

2) What's another word that means courage or spunk?_____

3) Is there an expression to describe an indirect way of getting someone to do something because you've spent money on them?_____

4) What is another way to say original and bizarre?_____

5) How can you say you're a natural at doing something?_____

■ **MAKE THIS MAKE SENSE:** Ask Student 2 to change these sentences to make sense.

1) Hey babe, let me wine and dine you at that great fast-food restaurant.

2) If you're an international business representative, the funkier you dress the better!

3) I'm sure my boss bought my usual story about being late because of the traffic.

4) Meryl Streep should never have given up her restaurant career because she sure isn't cut out for acting even though she has won several Oscars.

5) Bob showed a lot of guts when he let Lucy chase the punk who ripped off their luggage at the airport.

Questions to Ask Someone from Student Group 3

Ask Student 3 the following questions. He or she will tell you the answers. You should write down the answers. Student 3 can look at pages 6-7 to find the answers.

■ **TELL ME:** Ask Student 3 following questions to get the expressions.

1) How can you say you feel thrilled about something? _____

2) What do you call a materialistic and trendy person? _____

3) Is there a way to express that things will turn out fine? _____

4) To make a long story short, you can say _____

5) What's a way to say you're looking for trouble? _____

■ **MAKE THIS MAKE SENSE:** Ask Student 3 to change these sentences to make sense.

1) You won't be asking for it at all if you mouth off to a dictator.

2) You must not be very jazzed about winning the $1,000,000 lottery.

3) Well, in a nutshell, we began the morning by deciding what kind of juice to drink and cereal to eat. There were just so many choices! I felt like having some granola, but Joe wanted his boring old cornflakes. And then there was the juice dilemma: pulp or non-pulp...

4) The World Literature Appreciation class is full of yuppies.

5) Italian designers rarely make out very well in the fashion world.

PART III It's Halftime

Students 1—2—3

Before you begin the Halftime Activities, you must first complete pages 2-10. These activities are designed to get you to think about and discuss any extended meaning and use of the expressions you have just studied.

■ **EXPRESSION GUIDE:** With your classmates or with a native speaker, look at the Expression Guide below to find out if there is any information to add about the expressions. Write down anything interesting you discover. You can use some of the questions below to get started:

1. Do you or would you use these expressions? Why or why not?

2. Are there any other meanings related to the expressions?

3. Is there any special way to say these expressions?

4. Do you know how these expressions may have originated?

EXPRESSION GUIDE

give me a break	be straight *idiom/slang*	catch on	push your luck	the whole nine yards
guts	funky *slang*	don't buy it	be cut out for	wine and dine
yuppie	be jazzed	make out	be asking for it	in a nutshell

■ **FIND OUT MORE:** Below is more information about the meanings of some of the expressions as well as a few grammar tips.

1) **straight**—In addition to the idiomatic meanings we've studied: conventional or direct, **straight** has two very common slang meanings: (a) heterosexual; in other words, not gay, and (b) no longer involved in criminal activities. If you want to get something straight, it means that you want to make sure you understand something clearly. Let's see if you can get some of the meanings of **straight** by rewriting the following sentence:

Look, I have to be <u>straight</u> with you. Eduardo <u>isn't straight</u> and he hasn't told his family because they are very <u>straight</u>. He's afraid of how they might react.

2) **break**—**Break** is a word in English that is highly idiomatic, especially in terms of phrasal verbs (break up-down-out-in-through, etc). **Give me a break** means not only to be lenient with someone, but also has a slang meaning of to stop joking, kidding, or fooling someone. One more notable expression is **Those are the breaks**, which expresses the thought that life is tough or unfair sometimes and there is nothing you can do about it. Match the underlined expressions to their definitions.

Rudy couldn't go on the ski trip because his car <u>broke down</u> and he had to spend
(1)_____
the money he had saved for the trip to fix his car. The mechanic charged him a lot of money even though Rudy asked him to <u>give him a break</u>. When he told
(2)_____
his friends that he couldn't go, they said, "Come on bro, <u>give us a break</u>!" Rudy
(3)_____
replied, "Hey man, <u>those are the breaks</u>!
(4)_____

a) Are you kidding?   *b)* How about a discount?

c) malfunction   *d)* That's life. C'est la vie!

3) **catch**—**Catch** is another word with several interesting expressions worth mentioning. As a noun, **catch** has two meanings: (a) something inconvenient and unexpected; a **drawback**, and (b) a desirable person to marry. There is also a **catch-22**, which describes an impossible situation. As a verb, if you **get caught**, it means someone saw you doing something you shouldn't have been doing, such as speeding or drinking directly from, for example, the milk bottle, instead of pouring yourself a glass. If you **play catch up**, it means you are trying to stay with the competition or trying to recover lost time. Complete the sentences below by using different meanings of **catch**:

a) Our computer was down all morning, so I'm going to skip lunch because I have to _____ to get all the work done before 4:00.

b) Karen _____ smoking by her parents when she was 12 years old!

c) He's nice, well-educated, funny, healthy, and handsome, and he has a good job. What _____!

4) **buy it**—Because **buy it** is usually used in the negative (I don't buy it), when it is used in the affirmative, there is the impression that someone has been able

to successfully do something challenging. Sometimes people **buy into** what they see on TV; in other words, they accept what they see on TV to be true. Finally, it is a well-known fact that some people can **be bought**, be they judges, politicians, or even "fair weather friends." Complete the following with some idiomatic expression of **buy**:

a) I can't believe you _____ that scheme on the Internet. How much money did you send?

b) I'm so jazzed! They _____ my idea! I got the green light to get started on my proposal!

c) You can wine them and dine them, but you _____ them!

5) guts—To **have guts** means to have courage, and there are two related adjective forms: **gutsy**, which means to be audacious or plucky, and **gutless**, which means cowardly. As a noun, **gut** has two more interesting meanings: intuition—your **gut** feeling, and a big stomach or a potbelly—a big **gut**, usually from drinking too much beer (also called a beer belly). If you **spill your guts**, it means you share your most intimate or secret feelings. Complete the examples with the correct form of **gut** and match them to their definitions:

a) My _____ tells me not to go.____   *a)* beer belly

b) He finally _____ and told her he loves her.____   *b)* intuition

c) Murph, the pub owner, sure has _____.____   *c)* courageous

d) That was a pretty _____ move on your part.____   *d)* confess

6) funky—The most common meaning of **funky** is "unconventionally interesting" although there is also a pejorative meaning. If milk goes sour, it smells **funky**. If someone has a strange or unattractive accent, you could say they have a **funky** way of speaking. If someone says or does something that is unclear and strange, you could say that was **funky**. In a nutshell, funky can also mean unappealing. **FUNK** music is an earthy blues type of jazz music. To **be in a funk** means you're feeling depressed because you're having a difficult time. Fill in the sentences below with a correct form of these expressions.

a) I really liked that coat except for all the _____ flowers on the back._____

              meaning

b) Whenever I _____, I like to listen to _____ to get some of my energy back. _____

                                   meanings

7) make out—You learned that **make out** means in the positive sense to do well or succeed. Perhaps you already know the other popular meaning: to kiss and hug in a sexual way. Two other colorful ways to express this second meaning of **make out** are **to neck** and **to watch the submarine races**. There is one other meaning of **make out**: to be able to read, see, or hear something. Which meaning of **make out** is used in the sentences below?

a) It was raining so hard that I **couldn't make out** what the sign said, so we ended up driving 30 miles out of our way._____

b) You **had better not make out** at school because you'll get in trouble if you get caught._____

8) **yuppie**—In addition to the **yuppies**, there are also the **dinks**, the **baby boomers**, and **Generations X and Y**. **Dink** means "double income no kids" and refers to a couple who is more interested in accumulating material things than spending their income on a family. **Baby boomers** refer to a large generation of people born in the U.S. between 1946 and 1965. **Generation Xers** are often the children of **baby boomers**. **Generation Y** is an even younger group of people. They have grown up with computers and music television. Discuss.

■ Read the following and discuss the probable meanings of the underlined expressions. Circle any key words or phrases that help you to understand the meaning(s). Be sure to work with a partner.

1) Baby boomers, many of whom are yuppies and dinks, have a huge influence on the economy because, as a group, they have the greatest purchasing power and they are the largest body of voters. That's why most politicians try to appeal to this crowd when campaigning. President Clinton is the first baby boomer president, but he is neither a yuppie nor a dink.

2) Harold was simply not cut out for being a real estate agent. He was on an emotional roller coaster every time a customer would back out of a deal. He started drinking beer at lunch, and now he has quite a gut on him.

3) Come on! Are you for real? You want me to clean the refrigerator now? It's Saturday morning! Give me a break! You know I'm not cut out for this kind of work!

4) My gut is telling me that I should go for this new job although I'm not sure if I'm gutsy enough to make such a big change in my life. I'd have to move from San Diego to New York City!

5) I couldn't really make out what time they said they'd be arriving because the cell phone reception was so bad. I think I'd better wait awhile and call them back so I can get it straight.

6) Linda grew up in a small town and used to be very straight until she lived abroad and traveled for a few years. A lot of her old friends think she has developed some funky political views, but, in a nutshell, she doesn't care what they think because she finds that most of them have become yuppies.

7) I knew I was asking for it, but I had a gut feeling that I was going to win, so I kept pushing my luck playing blackjack. I wanted to win enough money to surprise my girlfriend by going the whole nine yards to wine and dine her at Bistro Bellagio. I'm glad I did because she was totally jazzed!

8) They're not going to buy your story about not having enough money to buy the textbooks when they catch you driving around in your brand new Jeep. Why don't you just buy the books?!

9) We <u>made out</u> very well at the meeting, but there was one <u>catch</u> in the negotiation: in order to win the contract, we have to do business exclusively with them until we reach the sales objective.

10) Steve is really <u>in a funk</u>. He has a golden opportunity to build his career, but he'll have to do a lot of traveling, and his girlfriend told him that she doesn't want a long-distance relationship. He really loves his girlfriend, and he doesn't want to make her unhappy. It's <u>a catch-22</u>.

■ **EXPRESSION LOG:** (1) Choose any 15 expressions from this chapter to practice by writing original sentences, then (2) add two new expressions that you hear. Follow the New Expression Guide in Appendix A.

■ **LISTEN** to the short stories. Select and write down the most suitable expressions along with any key words which helped you make your choice.

1.	2.	3.
_____ *expression* _____ *key words*	_____ *expression* _____ *key words*	_____ *expression* _____ *key words*
4.	5.	6.
_____ *expression* _____ *key words*	_____ *expression* _____ *key words*	_____ *expression* _____ *key words*
7.	8.	9.
_____ *expression* _____ *key words*	_____ *expression* _____ *key words*	_____ *expression* _____ *key words*
10.	11.	12.
_____ *expression* _____ *key words*	_____ *expression* _____ *key words*	_____ *expression* _____ *key words*
13.	14.	15.
_____ *expression* _____ *key words*	_____ *expression* _____ *key words*	_____ *expression* _____ *key words*

RULES:
- Roll the die: If the number is odd, choose one expression to use in a short story. (1 point)
  If the number is even, choose two expressions to use in a short story. (2 points)
- You must finish telling your story within one minute.
- If you can use a third expression in your story, it is worth 1 more point.
- Each expression may only be used twice, unless you specify that you're using an extended meaning. Check them off as they are used.
- The first person to reach 21 wins.

give me a break 1___ 2___	catch on 1___ 2___	be straight 1___ 2___	wine and dine 1___ 2___	be asking for it 1___ 2___
gut 1___ 2___	be cut out for 1___ 2___	don't buy it 1___ 2___	yuppie 1___ 2___	funky 1___ 2___
be jazzed 1___ 2___	make out 1___ 2___	guts 1___ 2___	push your luck 1___ 2___	those are the breaks 1___ 2___
play catch up 1___ 2___	in a funk 1___ 2___	babyboomers 1___ 2___	neck 1___ 2___	get caught 1___ 2___
buy into 1___ 2___	a catch-22 1___ 2___	get something straight 1___ 2___	in a nutshell 1___ 2___	the whole nine yards 1___ 2___

Keep Score

Name	Name	Name	Name

be cut out for

C H A P T E R

2

spaced out

a tip

have what it takes

schmooze

food for thought

a flake

get even

deal with

cut corners

speak of the devil

a wimp

keep\be up on

get away with

grow on someone

bend over backwards

Student Group 1

Learn the meanings of the following five expressions by completing the exercises. Work with Student Group 1 or by yourself.

■ **GUESS** the meanings of the five expressions.

1) Let me give you a tip: don't call him in the morning! You're better off waiting till the afternoon after he's eaten.

2) Karine arrived from Geneva a few days ago and she's still feeling a little spaced out from jet lag.

3) Luis got the Salesperson of the Month award. He sure has what it takes!

4) Christopher really knows how to schmooze; he can get anyone to reveal what they care about most within 15 minutes of talking to them.

5) Here's some food for thought: let's take six months off and travel around the States.

■ **CHECK OUT** the definitions and examples of the expressions.

1) tip—a suggestion or helpful information which is sometimes privileged, a hint.
Hey—thanks for the tip about how to use Windows 2000. It'll save me a lot of time and trouble!

2) spaced out—feeling out of touch with what's going on around you due to fatigue or stress; out of touch with reality, inability to concentrate; eccentric, weird.
Jack is my spaced-out neighbor. He can never remember where he parks his car, but he can provide you with vivid details about any war.

3) have what it takes—have the qualities or abilities necessary to be successful.
Do you have what it takes to become truly fluent in another language?

4) schmooze—the art of flattery, with or without ulterior motives.
Donna schmoozes everyone. That's why she gets so many discounts.

5) food for thought—information, ideas to reflect on, ponder.
We never watch movies on TV, so if we cancel the premium channels, we'll have some extra cash to upgrade our computer in a year. Now there's food for thought.

■ **QUICK FIX**—Match the expressions to the words that are similar.

1) competent   _____ schmooze

2) reflection   _____ spaced out

3) a clue   _____ food for thought

4) praise   _____ have what it takes

5) odd   _____ a tip

■ **CLOZE IT**—Use one of the above expressions to complete the sentences. Be sure to pay attention to any necessary grammatical changes.

1) Hey, your _____ is working. I'll do whatever you want!

2) Why didn't I think of that! What a great idea— that sure is _____!

3) Do you have any _____ about renting an apartment in this area?

4) I'm sorry. I _____ while you were talking. What did you say?

5) Carlos Santana definitely _____ to make it in the music industry!

■ **SENSE OR NONSENSE**—With your classmates, discuss the sentences and decide if they do or don't make sense.

1) Hillary Clinton doesn't have what it takes to be in politics._____

2) I'm feeling a little spaced out because I didn't sleep well._____

3) Sherlock Holmes is a master at exploiting tips._____

4) Einstein gave us plenty of food for thought about the universe._____

5) Look at all those Hollywood "wannabes" schmoozing for acting parts._____

■ **PLUG IT IN**—Use the expressions to replace the underlined words. Make sure to check your grammar! Check the Index/Glossary for words you may not know.

1) *Memoirs of a Geisha* was a great read, full of <u>a lot to contemplate</u>.

2) James <u>isn't with it</u> today. Maybe he doesn't feel well.

3) Here are a few <u>pointers</u> about how to set up your surround sound system.

4) Carlos <u>is the person</u> for the job. He's completely bilingual with loads of experience.

5) My boyfriend <u>gives me much too much credit</u>, but I don't mind.

Student Group 2

Learn the meanings of the following five expressions by completing the exercises. Work with Student Group 2 or by yourself.

■ **GUESS** the meanings of the five expressions.

1) I wouldn't count on Pat for that. You know what **a flake** he can be sometimes.

2) Don't get mad; **get even**!

3) How does Roxanne **deal with** so many people so effectively?

4) Let's find a way to **cut corners** on this so that we can save some time.

5) Well, look who's here. **Speak of the devil!**

■ **CHECK OUT** the definitions and examples of the expressions.

1) **a flake**—an unreliable person, odd or eccentric.
   Joe didn't come to the meeting again. He is such a flake!

2) **get even**—get revenge, pay back, punish.
   Don't worry. She'll get even with him for being such a flake.

3) **deal with**—manage, handle, control.
   Keiko gets sick easily. She can't deal with too much stress.

4) **cut corners**—find ways to make things easier and less time-consuming.
   Believe me. I have cut every corner I can and I can't do this any faster!

5) **speak of the devil**—all of a sudden the person you're thinking of or talking about makes some sort of appearance.
   Speak of the devil! I was just thinking about calling you!

■ **QUICK FIX**—Match the expressions to the words that are similar.

1) find shortcuts   _____speak of the devil

2) undependable   _____cut corners

3) retaliate   _____flake

4) coincidence   _____deal with

5) engage in   _____get even

■ **CLOZE IT**—Use one of the above expressions to complete the sentences. Be sure to pay attention to any necessary grammatical changes.

1) That's so weird. I just e-mailed you too! _____!

2) Larry is always _____, finding the easy way out.

3) Julie is _____ when it comes to being on time. In a nutshell, she was born late!

4) I know you were kidding, but I _____ with you when you least expect it.

5) Neal has a lot to _____ right now; he's moving and starting a new job!

■ **SENSE OR NONSENSE**—With your classmates, discuss the sentences and decide if they do or don't make sense.

1) Speak of the devil—It's Elvis Presley at a gas station again!_____

2) Dealing with too much is great for your blood pressure._____

3) Computers have really helped people cut corners._____

4) Don't mess with the mob. They may get even with you._____

5) Some of my most trusted friends are total flakes._____

■ **PLUG IT IN**—Use the expressions to replace the underlined words. Make sure to check your grammar! Check the Index/Glossary for words you may not know.

1) Let's not reinvent the wheel with this. Isn't there a better way?

2) Hey—I've got a score to settle with you. Look for me when you least expect it.

3) Look what the cat dragged in. I was wondering where you were.

4) I have plenty on my plate already, so give this assignment to someone else.

5) That doctor is a quack! He's not even a member of the American Medical Association.

Student Group 3

Learn the meanings of the following five expressions by completing the exercises. Work with Student Group 3 or by yourself.

■ **GUESS** the meanings of the five expressions.

1) Tim can't defend himself. He's too much of a wimp.

2) Henry has to keep up on the latest in his field. He's the boss!

3) Despite all the overwhelming evidence against him, the accused murderer got away with it and is a free man.

4) Diane seems to be growing on Jose. He never smiles except when he's around her.

5) Marie was putting in 12-hour days. She went out of her way and bent over backwards to make the new business work.

■ **CHECK OUT** the definitions and examples of the expressions.

1) a wimp—a very weak person; someone with no guts.
   I thought I could go skydiving, but I'm too much of a wimp.

2) keep/be up on—be informed about the latest information.
   David is always up on what's happening in the world. He's a "news junkie."

3) get away with—be able to do something that you shouldn't and not get in trouble for it.
   How is it that Bob always gets away with being late, but if I am, everyone seems to notice?

4) grow on someone—influence or impress someone in a positive way over time.
   Pam didn't notice him at first, but he slowly grew on her. They've started to see more and more of each other.

5) bend over backwards—inconvenience yourself to help someone else.
   I don't mind bending over backwards for my good friends.

■ **QUICK FIX**—Match the expressions to the words that are similar.

1) current   _____grow on someone

2) not be held accountable   _____a wimp

3) affect positively   _____bend over backwards

4) make a big effort   ____keep up on

5) coward   ____get away with

■ **CLOZE IT**—Use one of the above expressions to complete the sentences. Be sure to pay attention to any necessary grammatical changes.

1) I told you you'd get caught. How did you think you _____ that in the first place?

2) Maikel loves to _____ the latest surf report being the consummate surfer that he is.

3) She _____ me each time I hear her speak.

4) Are you kidding? He won't play football? He's too much of _____.

5) We're all going to have _____ to make this work. It'll be a team effort.

■ **SENSE OR NONSENSE**—With your classmates, discuss the sentences and decide if they do or don't make sense.

1) They grew on each other so much that they broke up._____

2) A lot of people try to get away with not paying taxes._____

3) Wimps always stand up for what they believe in._____

4) You can always trust a flaky person to bend over backwards for you._____

5) The CNN news crew has to be up on what's happening in the world._____

■ **PLUG IT IN**—Use the expressions to replace the underlined words. Make sure to check your grammar. Check the Index/Glossary for words you may not know.

1) They <u>pulled off</u> the bank robbery and rumor has it that they're now living the "big life" somewhere on the Caribbean.

2) Carmen has become <u>a chicken</u> ever since she broke her leg. She won't go skiing anymore. I can't say I blame her.

3) I really respect the way he thinks. I can tell he's <u>been rubbing off on me</u>.

4) You are so <u>knowledgeable about</u> what's going on in China! I didn't know any of that!

5) You really <u>went out of your way</u> for me. Thank you so much. I truly appreciate it.

Questions to Ask Someone from Student Group 1

Ask Student 1 the following questions. He or she will tell you the answers. You should write down the answers. Student 1 can look at pages 20-21 to find the answers.

■ **TELL ME:** Ask Student 1 the following questions to get the expressions.

1) Is there a similar expression to being cut out for something?_____

2) What is a way to say this is interesting to think about?_____

3) How can I say I feel strange because I'm tired?_____

4) What's another word for clue or hint?_____

5) Is there an expression which means to feed someone's ego?_____

■ **MAKE THIS MAKE SENSE:** Ask Student 1 to change these sentences to make sense.

1) Yuppies are always full of food for thought.

2) I hope Dr. White is spaced out when he performs my surgery.

3) Most people have what it takes to get into Harvard, Princeton, or Yale Universities.

4) Your do-it-yourself tip worked great. Now I have to call the plumber!

5) Schmoozing the cop always gets you out of a ticket.

Questions to Ask Someone from Student Group 2

Ask Student 2 the following questions. He or she will tell you the answers. You should write down the answers. Student 2 can look at pages 23-24 to find the answers.

■ **TELL ME:** Ask Student 2 the following questions to get the expressions.

1) What's a way to say you're going to get back at someone?_____

2) Is there a way to say there must be an easier and faster way to do something?___

3) How can I say I was just thinking about you and suddenly you're here?_____

4) What is an expression meaning to handle or control something?_____

5) Is there a word for someone who is odd or undependable?_____

■ **MAKE THIS MAKE SENSE:** Ask Student 2 to change these sentences to make sense.

1) Let's cut some corners and restart at zero.

2) Well, speak of the devil—I had forgotten all about you.

3) The mega-giant company America Online won't have to deal with much more customer service after the merger with Time Warner, another mega-giant.

4) Mr. Kovaks made it to the top because he is such a flake.

5) Sue got even with me when she didn't reveal my deep dark secret.

Questions to ASK Someone from Student Group 3

Ask Student 3 the following questions. He or she will tell you the answers. You should write down the answers. Student 3 can look at pages 25-27 to find the answers.

■ **TELL ME:** Ask Student 3 following questions to get the expressions.

1) What is an expression describing being able to do something without getting in trouble?_____

2) Is there another word for someone with no guts?_____

3) How can you say that you inconvenience yourself for someone else?_____

4) Is there an expression which means to stay current with something?_____

5) What is a way to say you become fond of someone slowly?_____

■ **MAKE THIS MAKE SENSE:** Ask Student 3 to change these sentences to make sense.

1) I won't bend over backwards for you, so I'll do whatever you need me to do.

2) The Vice-President of the U.S. isn't very up on what's happening in the American political parties.

3) Walter is a great catch. He's gotten away with being irresponsible his whole life. He'd make a wonderful husband.

4) Rie can't stand hanging out with him because he's growing on her.

5) Frank is too much of a wimp not to go deep sea diving.

PART III It's Halftime

Students 1—2—3

Before you begin the Halftime Activities, you must first complete pages 20-30. These activities are designed to get you to think about and discuss any extended meaning and use of the expressions you have just studied.

■ **EXPRESSION GUIDE:** With your classmates or with a native speaker, look at the Expression Guide below to find out if there is any information to add about the expressions. Write down anything interesting you discover. You can use some of the questions below to get started:

1. Do you use these expressions? Why or why not?

2. Are there any other meanings related to the expressions?

3. Is there any special way to say these expressions?

4. Do you know how these expressions may have originated?

EXPRESSION GUIDE

a tip	spaced out *slang*	have what it takes	schmooze *slang*	food for thought
a flake *slang*	get even	deal with	cut corners	speak of the devil
a wimp *slang*	keep/be up on	get away with	grow on someone	bend over backwards

■ **FIND OUT MORE:** Below is more information about the meanings of some of the expressions as well as a few grammar tips.

1) tip—In addition to **tip** meaning helpful or useful information or advice, the verb **tip off** means to reveal, or **give away**, information/evidence with or without intending to. For example, someone's red eyes could **tip you off** that that person may be tired or drunk. The police often receive anonymous calls that **tip them off**, which may help them do their job. Investigative journalists and salespeople also seek tips, which are called **sources** and **leads** respectively. Detectives use logic to piece together **clues or tips**. However, if you are **clueless**, this means you are ignorant or unaware. Finally, it's customary to **t.i.p.** (to insure promptness) people in the food, beverage, hotel, and esthetics industry in the U.S. Choose the appropriate synonym(s) or form(s) of **tip**:

   a) A real estate agent_____
   b) A reporter for the Wall Street Journal_____
   c) Sherlock Holmes_____
   d) A defense lawyer_____
   e) An ESL student_____
   f) A card dealer at Caesar's Palace in Las Vegas_____
   g) A stockbroker_____
   h) A hairdresser_____

2) have what it takes—If you **have what it takes**, then you **can take it**. This expression means you are able to put up with, tolerate, or deal with pressure or stress. So, if you can't take the heat, try **not to take it out on someone**. This means don't make someone else suffer because you are suffering. Complete the paragraph using the appropriate forms of take:

   Carl began to _____ his frustration with work _____ his wife. He _____ the intense sales competition every month without coming home and starting to drink. He needs to face that he _____ and look for another line of work.

3) flake—The noun **flake** has a related verb and adjective form: **flake out** and **flaky**. They basically describe unreliability, laziness, eccentricity, and oddness. Complete the situation below with the best form of **flake**:

   I'm sorry _____ on you guys, but I'm too tired to go. I don't mean to seem _____. I promise I'll go next time. You know I will because I'm not _____.

4) get even—A synonym for **get even** is even the score. But if you are **even steven**, that means you don't owe anything—that everything has been divided fairly and equally. If you even out something, it means you divide and distribute something fairly and equally. Complete the sentences below with a suitable form of even:

   a) What—you cheated playing cards again! That does it. We're going to _____ right now!
   b) We absolutely have to _____ this workload. It's not fair that some of us are working overtime while others aren't carrying their weight.
   c) Hey—don't I owe you something? Nope, we're _____.

5) **deal with**—**Deal** is a word that is highly idiomatic in English. Here are just a few more very common expressions, some of which you may already know. Discover the meanings!

a) I got a great deal on my computer!   _____what's the problem

b) (handshake) You've got a deal!   _____why is that so important?

c) So, what's the big deal?   _____don't be concerned

d) What's the deal with that?   _____agree

e) No big deal   _____a bargain

6) **up on**—You can be **up on, up front, up for, up to** and **up**. See if you can guess the meanings by matching them with these expressions.

a) Look, I have to be **up front** with you.   _____feel like, feel up to
     So please don't take this personally.

b) I know you just got back from your trip.   _____positive/happy
     Are you sure you're **up for** going dancing?

c) Don't worry. I was already **up**.   _____straight

d) Great—the computers are back **up**.   _____what's been happening

e) You should ask the boss today. He is   _____functioning, operating
     really **up**. He'll probably agree!

f) What have you been **up to** these days?   _____awake

7) **bend over backwards**—Sometimes if you **bend over backwards** for someone, but they take you for granted, you get **bent out of shape**. This means you feel so exasperated or disappointed that you can't hide your emotions. Check off what might make you get **all bent out of shape**:

a) Having to wait at the airport for an unspecified amount of time which will make you miss a very important meeting.   yes   no

b) Being told that you have to go back to your country because there was a mix-up with your immigration paperwork.   yes   no

c) Spending over $1,000 to have your car repaired and it breaks down a week later.   yes   no

8) **grow on someone**—Similar to **growing on someone**, if someone is **rubbing off on** you, that means you are being influenced in some way by that person, although it doesn't necessarily mean you are starting to like that person. However, if someone **rubs you the wrong way**, that means there is something about that person that **gets on your nerves**. You may not even know what it is about that person that you don't like; it could be something very surface. Use forms of **rub off** to complete the sentences:

a) I can tell that Jerry _____ you. He always says, "What's up with this...What's up with that," and I've noticed that you've been saying that quite a bit lately too.

b) We must have gotten off on the wrong foot or something, but there is something about Jill that _____. Maybe she just gets up on the wrong side of the bed...

■ Read the following and discuss the probable meanings of the underlined expressions. Circle any key words or phrases that help you to understand the meaning(s). It's best to work with a partner.

1) Allison has excellent front office skills: not only is she efficient and accurate, she's also capable of <u>dealing with</u> a wide variety of people in a friendly and consistent manner. Plus she's fast! She really knows how to <u>cut corners</u> and get the job done!

2) Glenna definitely has <u>what it takes</u> for her position as International Student Housing Coordinator. She even goes the extra mile by <u>bending over backwards</u> for people by providing them with all sorts of useful <u>tips</u> about life in the U.S.

3) I heard part of the City of San Diego Mayor's speech on the radio the other night, but I must admit <u>I'm not really up on</u> city politics. She was, however, talking about uniting more of the cities in the county, but she didn't mention anything about improving public transportation. I know many people wish San Diego had a subway system, but that would take forever and a day to negotiate. Here's <u>some food for thought</u>: why not build a train system that goes right along the center of the existing freeways?

4) Well, <u>speak of the devil</u>—I was just about to e-mail you again! I know I haven't been great at <u>staying in touch</u> either, but <u>we're even</u> now! Anyway, how's it going—<u>what's up</u> at work? The last I heard was...

5) Shigeko's been complaining that she's been studying so much that she feels totally <u>spaced out</u>, especially with all the reading she has to do. But, that's what you get for being in a doctorate program at UCLA! She's so <u>tough</u> on herself—if we don't make her take a break, nobody will. Why don't we <u>schmooze</u> her into going out for sushi and remind her that soon her friends may be calling her Dr. Shigeko!

6) Bruce got completely <u>bent out of shape</u> the other day with good reason: he contracted out some of the project to an old friend he was trying to help out, but the guy <u>flaked out</u> and didn't <u>come through</u> in time. As a result, Bruce missed his deadline and now has to reschedule a large portion of the project. "Never again," he said.

7) The problem with Bruce's old friend, Dan, is that he is used to <u>getting away with</u> taking advantage of people and never really accepting responsibility for his own actions or lack thereof. Bruce may be the first person to <u>be upfront</u> with him and tell him that he's not going to give him anymore work because he can't be <u>counted on</u>. This will definitely put a dent in the friendship, but it may be the best thing for Dan, who has to realize that being <u>flaky</u> is <u>a big deal</u> and has consequences.

8) Marie never <u>feels up to</u> doing anything lately because she says doesn't have energy. What she needs is to get some exercise, but her excuse is that she's too much of a <u>wimp</u> to do any sports. We think she should get an exercise bike. That way she could get some aerobic exercise and read, listen to music or the radio, or watch TV at the same time.

9) A little bit of Kim <u>rubs off on</u> almost everyone who meets her because she has extraordinary people skills. That's just one reason she is so busy: every day so many people <u>drop by</u> her office seeking her advice. It's amazing how she <u>can take</u> the constant interruptions and still get her work done!

10) He's <u>growing on</u> her more and more every day with his kind, thoughtful and funny ways. She feels lucky!

■ **EXPRESSION LOG:** (1) Choose any 15 expressions from this chapter to practice by writing original sentences, then (2) add two new expressions that you hear. Follow the New Expression Guide in Appendix A.

1) Listen and write down the expression(s) you hear.

2) Decide if the sentences make sense or not (yes or no).

3) Explain why the expression was or was not used in a meaningful way.

Expression(s)	Yes or No	Explanation
1.		
2.		
3.		
4.		
5.		
6.		
7.		
8.		
9.		
10.		
11.		
12.		

RULES:
- Roll the die. If the number is:
  ODD 1, 3, 5: Choose an expression and use it to TELL us something.
  EVEN 2, 4, 6: Choose an expression and use it to ASK a classmate something.
- Write your name next to the O_____! or the E_____?
- Use each expression one time only for each ODD or EVEN roll.

get even O _____ ! E _____ ?	grow on someone O _____ ! E _____ ?	food for thought O _____ ! E _____ ?	clueless O _____ ! E _____ ?	cut corners O _____ ! E _____ ?
have what it takes O _____ ! E _____ ?	schmooze O _____ ! E _____ ?	spaced out O _____ ! E _____ ?	a wimp O _____ ! E _____ ?	bent out of shape O _____ ! E _____ ?
deal with O _____ ! E _____ ?	rub someone the wrong way O _____ ! E _____ ?	bend over backwards O _____ ! E _____ ?	get away with O _____ ! E _____ ?	up on O _____ ! E _____ ?
a tip O _____ ! E _____ ?	feel up to O _____ ! E _____ ?	no big deal O _____ ! E _____ ?	even out O _____ ! E _____ ?	flake out O _____ ! E _____ ?

bend over backwards

3

the ball's in your court

play it by ear

a rain check

uptight

off the hook

go out on

off the wall

tailgate

bring up

bite off more than you can chew

wisecracks

set up

a drag

on the level

burned out

Work It Out

Student Group 1

Learn the meanings of the following five expressions by completing the exercises. Work with Student Group 1 or by yourself.

■ **GUESS** the meanings of the five expressions.

1) Since we don't know how the weather will be this weekend, let's **play it by ear**.

2) The electricity went out during the movie, so the theater gave us **a rain check**.

3) All the work I had to do made me feel **uptight**.

4) I thought I missed the meeting, but it got rescheduled anyway, so I'm **off the hook**.

5) The air conditioner keeps **going out** on us. It's time for a new one!

■ **CHECK OUT** the definitions and examples of the expressions.

1) **play it by ear**—do things as they happen, be spontaneous.
We had a fun and relaxing vacation because we decided to play it by ear.

2) **a rain check**—a free ticket to something or a guarantee to get something at a later date.
The store manager gave us a rain check for the chairs that were supposed to be in stock. We'll get some when the next shipment arrives.

3) **uptight**—nervous, tense, annoyed.
Edith gets really uptight whenever the computers go down.

4) **off the hook**—get out of an awkward situation, not be held responsible, out of trouble.
Robin didn't make it to the dinner, so she asked Tina to get her off the hook by saying that they got stuck in Los Angeles if she saw the people who invited her .

5) **go out on**—stop functioning; be unfaithful to someone, cheat on.
John went out on his girlfriend again, and she found out. I wonder what she's going to do?

■ **QUICK FIX**—Match the expressions to the words that are similar.

1) improvise   _____a rain check

2) disloyal   _____be off the hook

3) high strung   _____play it by ear

4) postpone   _____uptight

5) not in hot water   _____go out on

■ **CLOZE IT**—Use one of the above expressions to complete the sentences. Be sure to pay attention to any necessary grammatical changes.

1) What? No more hot water already? Has the water heater _____ us?

2) I sometimes get _____ if someone cancels at the last minute when they could have told me earlier.

3) I'm tired of planning. Why don't we _____ for a change?

4) The game was canceled, so we all got _____.

5) Joe _____ this time, but if he does it again he'll be pushing his luck.

■ **SENSE OR NONSENSE**—With your classmates, discuss the sentences and decide if they do or don't make sense.

1) We had a really tight schedule, so we could play it by ear._____

2) They gave us a rain check, so we'll never get to see it now!_____

3) Don't worry. I won't hold it against you. You're off the hook._____

4) Elena is a very easy-going and uptight person._____

5) My knee just went out on me, so I can play really well now._____

■ PLUG IT IN—Use the expressions to replace the underlined words. Make sure to check your grammar! Check the Index/Glossary for words you may not know.

1) Lee <u>could get away with it</u> this time, but he'd better be more careful next time.

2) Bill knew there was something wrong in his relationship when he started to feel like <u>dating other women instead of</u> his girlfriend.

3) Here's <u>a guarantee</u> that you'll get the next one as soon as it arrives.

4) Let's <u>see how they feel when they arrive</u>. After they get here, we'll all decide.

5) Kazu got <u>irritated</u> when his order arrived late for the third time in a row.

Student Group 2

Learn the meanings of the following five expressions by completing the exercises. Work with Student Group 2 or by yourself.

■ **GUESS** the meanings of the five expressions.

1) Jim Carrey, the comic actor, can get away with being as off the wall as he pleases.

2) I'd better change lanes—I'm being tailgated!

3) I hate to bring it up again, but we have got to finish this!

4) No wonder you're exhausted! You always bite off more than you can chew.

5) Hey—no wisecracks about my hair. I know I need to find a new barber.

■ **CHECK OUT** the definitions and examples of the expressions.

1) off the wall—nonsensical, eccentric, bizarre.
   Erik sent me a really off-the-wall e-mail joke. I'll forward it to you.

2) tailgate—drive behind someone too closely.
   We're not in a hurry—so don't tailgate!

3) bring up—mention; raise or educate.
   Margaret was brought up in a Catholic orphanage.

4) bite off more than you can chew—do more than you are capable of.
   Ralph thought he could install the cable himself, but he bit off more than he could chew. He needs to ask for help.

5) wisecracks—sarcastic, witty remarks, sometimes funny—sometimes not.
   David Letterman, a comedian and host of a late-night talk show, has made so many wisecracks about Hollywood legend Elizabeth Taylor that she will never come on his show.

■ **QUICK FIX**—Match the expressions to the words that are similar.

1) follow too closely   _____bite off more than you can chew

2) clever comeback   _____bring up

3) weird   _____tailgate

4) overwork   _____wisecracks

5) introduce new topic   _____off the wall

■ **CLOZE IT**—Use one of the above expressions to complete the sentences. Be sure to pay attention to any necessary grammatical changes.

1) Come on—let that idiot _____ pass you! It'll be safer!

2) That movie was so _____ that a few people left before it ended.

3) He shouldn't have taken on that assignment because now he _____.

4) Sorry to _____ Jean's name again, but she was the last person to use this.

5) All right, cut out the _____. I get your point.

■ **SENSE OR NONSENSE**—With your classmates, discuss the sentences and decide if they do or don't make sense.

1) Mike has plenty of time since he bit off more than he can chew._____

2) People often tailgate in the passing lane._____

3) It's great to be brought up in a big city._____

4) The new CEO is very off the wall._____

5) A business conference is the best place to make wisecracks._____

■ **PLUG IT IN**—Use the expressions to replace the underlined words. Make sure to check your grammar! Check the Index/Glossary for words you may not know.

1) Comedian Jerry Seinfeld always has some great <u>comebacks</u> whenever he does live shows.

2) I <u>was raised in</u> Southern California.

3) That guy is <u>right on my bumper</u>, but I can't get over!

4) Many people adore Robin Williams' <u>eccentric</u> sense of humor.

5) Better get some rest! <u>You're burning the candle at both ends</u>!

Student Group 3

Learn the meanings of the following five expressions by completing the exercises. Work with Student Group 3 or by yourself.

■ **GUESS** the meanings of the five expressions.

1) George set up a meeting with his boss so that I could tell him about our services.

2) I got a speeding ticket. What a drag!

3) The ball's in your court this time. You can take it any direction you choose.

4) Roxanne is a great boss because she is on the level with everyone.

5) Pascal needs at least a month off in order not to get burned out.

■ **CHECK OUT** the definitions and examples of the expressions.

1) set up—make arrangements for; put together, start.
   Gary can't wait to get home to set up his new computer!

2) a drag—uncomfortable, irritating or inconvenient situation or person.
   Neil is such a drag to go out with because he never tries to talk to anyone.

3) the ball's in your court—it's your decision, your move.
   I told you what I wanted. The ball's in your court now.

4) on the level—honest, trustworthy, legitimate, frank.
   You'll get Frank's real opinion because he's on the level.

5) burned out—feel mentally or emotionally exhausted.
   Alberto gets burned out whenever he bites off more than he can chew.

■ **QUICK FIX**—Match the expressions to the words that are similar.

1) a bummer   _____the ball's in your court

2) up to you   _____set up

3) straight   _____burn out

4) provide   _____a drag

5) no energy   _____on the level

■ **CLOZE IT**—Use one of the above expressions to complete the sentences. Be sure to pay attention to any necessary grammatical changes.

1) Richard's parents _____ with enough money to go to school without having to work.

2) Working on the weekends is _____!

3) Camila has to make the offer. _____.

4) You can be _____ with him. He's very open-minded.

5) She is getting _____ from the constant interruptions.

■ **SENSE OR NONSENSE**—With your classmates, discuss the sentences and decide if they do or don't make sense.

1) Setting up a business takes time and money._____

2) My car broke down again. What a drag!_____

3) I love to go to work whenever I feel burned out._____

4) It's important to be on the level about your physical condition with your doctor._____

5) The ball's in Mr. Wishy-Washy's court. I'm sure he'll make a move soon._____

■ **PLUG IT IN**—Use the expressions to replace the underlined words. Make sure to check your grammar! Check the Index/Glossary for words you may not know.

1) Fabi would be a good person to consult because she <u>doesn't beat around the bush</u>.

2) <u>It's your call</u>. Whatever you decide is fine.

3) Karl <u>has no more energy for</u> selling insurance. I think he needs a long vacation.

4) Carlos would like to <u>establish</u> a language school in Madrid.

5) Sitting around waiting with nothing to do is <u>the pits</u>.

Questions to Ask Someone from Student Group 1

Ask Student 1 the following questions. He or she will tell you the answers.
You should write down the answers. Student 1 can look at pages 40-42 to find
the answers.

■ **TELL ME:** Ask Student 1 the following questions to get the expressions.

1) What is a way to say that you want to be spontaneous?_____

2) How can you say that something has stopped working?_____

3) Is there a way to say you're not going to be in trouble?_____

4) What's another word for annoyed or nervous?_____

5) If someone offers something they can't provide at the time, what can they give
you instead?_____

■ **MAKE THIS MAKE SENSE:** Ask Student 1 to change these sentences
to make sense.

1) I'd love to get married to someone who'd go out on me.

2) The cop told her she was off the hook for speeding and promptly wrote up
the ticket.

3) We didn't get a rain check because they guaranteed to have one for every
customer.

4) I never feel uptight when I miss my plane.

5) Politicians love to play it by ear whenever they have official visits overseas.

Questions to Ask Someone from Student Group 2

Ask Student 2 the following questions. He or she will tell you the answers.
You should write down the answers. Student 2 can look at pages 43-44 to find
the answers.

■ **TELL ME:** Ask Student 2 the following questions to get the expressions.

1) What do you call someone who drives too closely behind you?_____

2) Is there another word for a sharp remark?_____

3) How can you say that you made yourself too busy?_____

4) What's another way to say that something or someone is weird?_____

5) How can you begin to talk about something because of the direction of the
conversation? _____

■ **MAKE THIS MAKE SENSE:** Ask Student 2 to change these sentences
to make sense.

1) Super straight people usually love to watch off-the-wall movies because they
get the humor.

2) I bit off more than I can chew at work, so I have time for a two-hour massage
today.

3) It's great when a huge truck is tailgating you in your little convertible.

4) Satomi doesn't enjoy working in the office because of all the funny wisecracks.

5) People brought up in very small towns are often quite open-minded when it
comes to trying new types of food.

Questions to Ask Someone from Student Group 3

Ask Student 3 the following questions. He or she will tell you the answers.
You should write down the answers. Student 3 can look at pages 45-46 to find
the answers.

■ **TELL ME:** Ask Student 3 following questions to get the expressions.

1)   What's a way to tell someone to make up their mind?_____

2)   Is there another word for "bummer" or "too bad"?_____

3)   What's another way to say someone is straight and to the point?_____

4)   How can I say I have zero energy because I'm sick of doing something?_____

5)   What's a way to say you can arrange something for someone?_____

■ **MAKE THIS MAKE SENSE:** Ask Student 3 to change these sentences
to make sense.

1)   The ball's in your court Steve. So go ahead—be a wimp.

2)   Organized crime is always on the level when it comes to business investments.

3)   The best thing to do when you're burned out from studying is hit the books.

4)   I'm so jazzed—I have lots of free time this weekend! What a drag!

5)   Traditional parents usually don't try to set up their children with potential
     marriage partners.

Students 1—2—3

Before you begin the Halftime Activities, you must first complete pages 40-49. These activities are designed to get you to think about and discuss any extended meaning and use of the expressions you have just studied.

■ **EXPRESSION GUIDE:** With your classmates or with a native speaker, look at the Expression Guide below to find out if there is any information to add about the expressions. Write down anything interesting you discover. You can use some of the questions below to get started:

1. Do you use these expressions? Why or why not?

2. Are there any other meanings related to the expressions?

3. Is there any special way to say these expressions?

4. Do you know how these expressions may have originated?

EXPRESSION GUIDE

play it by ear	a rain check	uptight *slang*	off the hook	go out on
off the wall *slang*	tailgate	bring up	bite off more than you can chew	wisecracks
set up	a drag *slang*	the ball's in your court	on the level	burned out

■ **FIND OUT MORE:** Below is more information about the meanings of some of the expressions as well as a few grammar tips.

1) play it by ear—"**Play it**" is used in a few other idiomatic expressions: **play it safe**, **play it cool** and **play it straight**. Write a definition for the expressions based on the examples below:

   a) Since we don't know how the weather is going to be, let's **<u>play it safe</u>** and bring our snow gear.

   _____

b) I know it's an uncomfortable situation, but just **play it cool**. Things will go more smoothly then.

_____

c) If you get audited by the Internal Revenue Service, you'd better **play it straight** or else you could end up paying a lot of penalties.

_____

2) off the hook—There are four more frequently used expressions containing some form of the word "hook": You can **be hooked on** caffeine, motorcycles, funk music, etc. If someone wants to **hook up with** you, they want to get together with you for business or social reasons. Sometimes students in California like to **play hooky** and go to the beach instead of school. The slang expression **hooker** refers to a female prostitute and is pejorative. Fill in the blanks below using the expressions containing **hook**:

a) Kids around the world _____ Pokémon.

b) In the movie *Pretty Woman*, Julia Roberts played _____ in Los Angeles.

c) My colleague said he would _____ us at the conference.

d) There's fresh powder on the ski slopes! Let's _____ today.

3) wisecracks—This expression, as well as its slang counterpart **wiseguy**, can be used in a fun or serious way depending on your intonation. You might enjoy joking with people who you know well by being a **wiseguy** who makes **wisecracks** about, for example, their driving or eating habits. A **wiseguy** could be a prankster or someone who likes to play practical jokes on people. On the other hand, if the situation is serious, calling someone a **wiseguy** means that you think someone is being flippant or too sarcastic. In that case, you may want to tell that person to **wise up**, which means to make someone become aware of something that they may not know because they are ignorant or they don't want to face reality. It could also mean that you want them to stop being obnoxious or irresponsible. Read the following sentences to decide which ones could be said with a joking or serious intonation pattern. Then, ask your teacher to demonstrate this intonation difference.

a) Way to go **wiseguy**! You almost killed me!_____

b) All right, knock it off. I've had enough of your **wisecracks**. When are you going to learn to be nice?_____

c) Who's the **wiseguy** that toilet-papered my desk? I'm going to get even with you, whoever you are!_____

d) She'd better **wise up** and face the fact that he's not going to change!_____

4) set up—This expression is highly idiomatic and requires further explanation in terms of its meaning and grammar. First of all, it is a transitive phrasal verb, which means it is also separable: We **set** the stereo **up** or we **set up** the stereo. In addition to the meanings we've studied, set up can also mean to arrange to put someone in a dangerous situation or dishonestly plan something for a specific result. The noun counterpart, **setup**, can likewise mean an arrangement, a false accusation, or a fraudulent scheme. Use a form of **set up** to complete the examples below:

a) The innocent man went to prison for life because he_____.

b) I really like your new office. It's a great_____.

c) Robert's parents _____ very comfortably for the rest of his life.

d) Be careful if you play poker with those guys. It's usually a big _____.

5) **a drag**—Check out more expressions containing **drag**. You've probably heard a few of these. See if you can match the examples to their meanings.

a) Is that a Cuban cigar? Can I have **a drag**?_____ **1)** procrastinate, be slow

b) He's a cross-dresser. He loves to dress in **drag** when his wife isn't home. **2)** force someone to confess or admit something.

c) The **drag queen** shows in West Hollywood, a gay city, are really entertaining. **3)** puff or inhale

d) Even though she saw him wearing her clothes, she still had to **drag** the truth **out of** him._____ **4)** male homosexuals dressed as women

e) Quit **dragging your feet** about doing your homework._____ **5)** men wearing women's clothes

6) **burned out**—The participle adjective **burned out** has a phrasal verb and noun counterpart. The phrasal verb **burn out** means not only to exhaust, but also to destroy by overheating or to stop functioning. The noun **burnout** refers to someone who has no more energy due to overwork or too much stress. Fill in the blanks below by using an appropriate form of **burned out**.

a) Omar _____ the brakes on his car because he never got the pads replaced.

b) Jean chose early retirement because she _____ from working so many years.

c) Paul is _____. He's not cut out for that high-stress sales position.

■ **READ** the following and discuss the probable meanings of the underlined expressions. Circle any key words or phrases that help you to understand the meaning(s). It's best to work with a partner.

1) All this road construction in the morning makes a lot of people get <u>uptight</u> as they drive to work, but you'd better not <u>tailgate</u> or else you're <u>setting yourself up</u> for trouble. Just <u>play it safe</u> and leave a few minutes earlier in the morning.

2) I know Mike is learning how to drive a stick shift, but we'd better tell him not to ride the clutch so he doesn't <u>burn it out</u>. That would be <u>a drag</u> to have to get it replaced!

3) I'm going to have to take <u>a rain check</u> tonight. I'm afraid <u>I've bitten off more than I can chew</u>. I have to stay at the office late to get this work done. How about getting together next week? I promise I won't <u>flake out</u> on you!

4) I'll let that <u>wisecrack</u> you made about my spaghetti sauce slide this time, but next time you won't get <u>off the hook</u> so easily.

5) Carlos was <u>brought up</u> in both the U.S. and Spain. That's the reason he is totally <u>hooked on</u> American football and Spanish folk music.

6) It was raining so hard last Saturday evening that the electricity <u>went out on</u> our entire block. We were planning on having a little dinner party, but we decided to <u>play it by ear</u>. Fortunately, we had plenty of candles, and it <u>turned out</u> to be quite the <u>setup</u>: not only did we have a wonderful candlelit atmosphere, but we also ended up cooking the old-fashioned way. We had <u>a blast</u>!

7) "Priscilla, Queen of the Desert" is a heartwarming, <u>off-the-wall</u> movie from Australia about a group of <u>drag queens</u> who take a roadtrip through the outback.

8) Lucy is getting really <u>burned out</u> from having to <u>drag everything out of you</u>. Why can't you <u>play it straight</u> with her and tell her what you really think?

9) OK—OK—I'll <u>set you up</u> with him if you really want me to, but <u>the ball's in your court</u> after that. I've told you that I don't think you two will have very much in common, so don't blame me if you don't like him—OK?

10) I know there are great sets of waves <u>rolling in</u>, but you'd better <u>wise up</u> and stop <u>playing hooky</u> to go surfing or else you're going to fail this class. Your <u>folks</u> won't be too thrilled about that!

■ **EXPRESSION LOG:** (1) Choose any 15 expressions from this chapter to practice by writing original sentences, then (2) add two new expressions that you hear. Follow the New Expression Guide in Appendix A.

- Listen to the stories and number #____ the box of expressions that best corresponds.
- Write down any key words.
- Decide how the story was told: Pleased___ Neutral___ Serious___

#____ P____ N____ S____ **off the wall, bring up, wisecracks**	#____ P____ N____ S____ **be hooked on, drag it out of you**
#____ P____ N____ S____ **burned out, tailgate, play it safe**	#____ P____ N____ S____ **on the level, the ball's in your court, set up**
#____ P____ N____ S____ **a drag, play it by ear, uptight**	#____ P____ N____ S____ **bring up, a rain check**
#____ P____ N____ S____ **drag my feet, bite off more than I can chew, play it cool**	#____ P____ N____ S____ **wise up, go out on, bite off more than he can chew, off the hook**
#____ P____ N____ S____ **play it safe, set up, go out on**	#____ P____ N____ S____ **play it straight, a drag, burned out**

Starting at 1, roll the die and move ahead to the corresponding box. Write your name(s) in the box. Go to the question with the same number and answer it using the expression indicated. Continue from your first roll around the board and answer all the questions. Use the boxes in which you write your name as your place marker.

1. _____ _____ **Names**	2. _____ _____ **Names**	3. _____ _____ **Names**	4. _____ _____ **Names**	5. _____ _____ **Names**
6. _____ _____ **Names**	7. _____ _____ **Names**	8. _____ _____ **Names**	9. _____ _____ **Names**	10. _____ _____ **Names**
11. _____ _____ **Names**	12. _____ _____ **Names**	13. _____ _____ **Names**	14. _____ _____ **Names**	15. _____ _____ **Names**

1) Describe a time when you got **off the hook** for something you did or when you **let someone off the hook** for something they did.

2) Do you like to **play it by ear** on vacation or do you prefer to plan your activities?

3) Who do you think is an **off-the-wall** person? Explain.

4) If someone you are seeing **goes out on you**, would you let them off the hook or would you **drag the truth out of them**?

5) What do you do for yourself when you feel **burned out**?

6) Describe a time when **the ball was in your court**—it was your move!

7) Do you know someone who makes a lot of **wisecracks**? Describe what that person says and does.

8) Have you ever **bitten off more than you can chew**? What did you do?

9) Tell us about the last time you felt **uptight**. What happened?

10) When was the last time you had to take **a rain check**? What was it for?

11) Have you ever heard of **a tailgate party**? Would you like to go to one?

12) Have your friends ever **set you up** with someone?

13) Do you think it's important to be **on the level** all the time? Explain.

14) Where were you **brought up**? Give a description.

15) Do you think it's **a drag** to do homework on the weekend?

uptight

4

tacky

Student Group 1

Learn the meanings of the following five expressions by completing the exercises. Work with Student Group 1 or by yourself.

■ **GUESS** the meanings of the five expressions.

1) The bottom line is that he has no choice; he has to move.

2) That was really tacky of Keith to ask personal questions at the business meeting.

3) Gary almost bought the house, but he decided to hold out for a better price.

4) Ok—twist my arm. Make me eat dessert!

5) So far, so good. We are clicking!

■ **CHECK OUT** the definitions and examples of the expressions.

1) the bottom line—the final decision, the truth, conclusion.
   When I buy a car, I want the bottom line price.

2) tacky—inappropriate; tasteless, overly decorated.
   Old Las Vegas is full of tacky hotels and casinos.

3) hold out—wait for something better, not give up, not give what is expected.
   The workers held out for two weeks until management agreed to negotiate.

4) twist someone's arm—convince or force someone to do something, usually in a joking way.
   Can I twist your arm and talk you into going dancing tonight? It'll be fun!

5) click—get along well, understand or perceive clearly.
   I'd been studying and studying, then all of a sudden it clicked. It made sense.

■ **QUICK FIX**—Match the expressions to the words that are similar.

1) tasteless   _____twist someone's arm

2) get it   _____the bottom line

3) persuade   _____click

4) don't quit   _____tacky

5) reality   _____hold out

■ **CLOZE IT**—Use one of the above expressions to complete the sentences. Be sure to pay attention to any necessary grammatical changes.

1) We woke up feeling tired Sunday morning, then next thing I knew he _____ _____ and we were off on a motorcycle ride in the desert!

2) _____ is that Scott just isn't a very nice person!

3) Mary decided to _____ until things were the way she wanted.

4) That restaurant has great food, but the decor is so _____.

5) It wouldn't be a very good idea to put them in the same office because they _____.

■ **SENSE OR NONSENSE**—With your classmates, discuss the sentences and decide if they do or don't make sense.

1) That conservative businesswoman wears the tackiest clothes._____

2) John held out for the best price and took the first one offered._____

3) This is the bottom line: what you see is what you get._____

4) Julia broke up with her boyfriend because they just didn't click._____

5) Let's see if I can twist your arm and talk you into going swimming._____

■ **PLUG IT IN**—Use the expressions to replace the underlined words. Make sure to check your grammar! Check the Index/Glossary for words you may not know.

1) Peter thought it would be best to <u>wait</u> in case we got more information before we made an offer.

2) I can't believe I let him <u>talk me</u> into going mountain biking again!

3) Just give <u>it to me straight</u>.

4) That's it! Finally, something <u>makes sense</u>!

5) That is the <u>ugliest</u> tie you've ever worn!

Student Group 2

Learn the meanings of the following five expressions by completing the exercises. Work with Student Group 2 or by yourself.

■ **GUESS** the meanings of the five expressions.

1) It's tax time! What a hassle! There are so many forms to fill out!

2) You'd better read the report and get the facts straight or else you may be off base.

3) I snoozed on my desk this afternoon after such a big lunch.

4) My credit card is maxed out, so I can't use it anymore.

5) We really hit it off. We've been seeing each other a lot lately.

■ **CHECK OUT** the definitions and examples of the expressions.

1) hassle—inconvenience, trouble; bother, disagree.
   My dad is hassling me about what I'm going to do after I finish high school.

2) off base—very mistaken; inappropriate.
   Your comment about her weight was way off base.

3) snooze—sleep, sleep lightly, nap.
   I usually hit the snooze button on my alarm clock so that I can sleep as much as possible.

4) max out—to reach the limit.
   Mike worked 70 hours this week. He must be maxed out.

5) hit it off—become fond of each other quickly, have a lot in common.
   Manuel and Caroline hit it off so well that they got married four months after they met.

■ **QUICK FIX**—Match the expressions to the words that are similar.

1) wrong   _____snooze

2) siesta   _____off base

3) strong liking _____max out

4) the peak   _____hassle

5) annoy   _____hit it off

■ **CLOZE IT**—Use one of the above expressions to complete the sentences. Be sure to pay attention to any necessary grammatical changes.

1) I'm _____ after driving ten hours straight. It's your turn.

2) Ugh—we have to fill out this form, then that form... What _____!

3) He was really _____ thinking he could schmooze her into donating more money.

4) Look at Bob _____ in front of the TV again.

5) I have a very good feeling about this company. It seems we _____.

■ **SENSE OR NONSENSE**—With your classmates, discuss the sentences and decide if they do or don't make sense.

1) After a big meal, I love to snooze for a little while._____

2) It was no hassle at all to disassemble the defective computer and return it._____

3) Many new credit card users max their cards out._____

4) Many people think the president's personal behavior has been way off base._____

5) The U.S. and Cuba have really been hitting it off recently._____

■ **PLUG IT IN**—Use the expressions to replace the underlined words. Make sure to check your grammar! Check the Index/Glossary for words you may not know.

1) The first time Tim and I met we <u>had a great conversation</u>, and we've been friends ever since.

2) He <u>has reached the point of no return</u>. You won't be able to change his mind now.

3) This whole thing is a <u>ridiculous mess</u>. Who is going to fix it?

4) There he is, basking in the sun and <u>snoring in never-never land.</u>

5) It cost us much more than we had originally thought. We <u>missed the boat</u> with our calculations!

Student Group 3

Learn the meanings of the following five expressions by completing the exercises. Work with Student Group 3 or by yourself.

■ **GUESS** the meanings of the five expressions.

1) There were almost no Y2K glitches like so many people had expected.

2) Ask Joan. She'll know. She's savvy about these things.

3) Shin picked up English so quickly that he finished the program in three quarters.

4) Wow—a free trip to Hawaii! You can't beat that!

5) When Antonio sees the new BMW bike, he's going to flip!

■ **CHECK OUT** the definitions and examples of the expressions.

1) glitch—technical error, flaw.
There's a little mark on all these copies. The copy machine must have a glitch.

2) savvy—having a combination of knowledge, logic, common sense, and cool.
Jose is very savvy about motorcycles. He can tell you whatever you want to know.

3) pick up—learn indirectly; flirt with someone.
Dancing is a popular way to pick up on girls.

4) can't be beat/can't beat that—that is the best.
A New York pizza just can't be beat.

5) flip (out)—become very excited, crazy, or angry.
When your dad sees what you did to his car, he is going to flip.

■ **QUICK FIX**—Match the expressions to the words that are similar.

1) know-how   _____pick up

2) freak out   _____be savvy

3) malfunction   _____can't be beat

4) catch on   _____flip

5) number 1   _____glitch

■ **CLOZE IT**—Use one of the above expressions to complete the sentences. Be sure to pay attention to any necessary grammatical changes.

1) *Silence of the Lambs* _____! It was the best horror movie ever.

2) Elizabeth is very _____ about grammar. She knows it inside out.

3) Christopher _____ some French during his vacation in France.

4) Rie is going to _____ at her surprise birthday party!

5) There was one minor _____ with the new equipment, but it's covered under the warranty.

■ **SENSE OR NONSENSE**—With your classmates, discuss the sentences and decide if they do or don't make sense.

1) Bars with dancing are usually a pick-up scene._____

2) There's a glitch with my printer because the footer doesn't print out clearly._____

3) The Pope, the head of the Roman Catholic Church, is always flipping out._____

4) Savvy people can become experts in some fields._____

5) American junk food can't be beat!_____

■ **PLUG IT IN**—Use the expressions to replace the underlined words. Make sure to check your grammar! Check the Index/Glossary for words you may not know.

1) The camera or film must <u>be flawed</u> because I normally get high-resolution pictures.

2) This new music <u>is awesome</u>. I could never get tired of listening to it!

3) Jean-Jacques <u>wrote the book on</u> wine. Let him choose it.

4) I <u>lost control</u> when they told us our plane had been canceled again!

5) He loves to <u>hit on</u> women in cafes.

Questions to Ask Someone from Student Group 1

Ask Student 1 the following questions. He or she will tell you the answers. You should write down the answers. Student 1 can look at pages 58-59 to find the answers.

■ **TELL ME:** Ask Student 1 the following questions to get the expressions.

1) How can I say that I want to wait until I get what I want?_____

2) What is a way to describe something that is tasteless or off color?_____

3) Is there a way to jokingly convince someone to do something?_____

4) What's a way to say give it to me straight?_____

5) What is an expression that means that everything seems to fit?_____

■ **MAKE THIS MAKE SENSE:** Ask Student 1 to change these sentences to make sense.

1) When I get married, I hope my wedding will be as tacky as possible.

2) He didn't twist my arm so well that I went wherever he wanted to go.

3) I can't stand this guy. We are really clicking. He's definitely growing on me!

4) The bottom line is open to interpretation.

5) They met each other one week and got married the next. They really held out.

Questions to Ask Someone from Student Group 2

Ask Student 2 the following questions. He or she will tell you the answers. You should write down the answers. Student 2 can look at pages 60-61 to find the answers.

■ **TELL ME:** Ask Student 2 the following questions to get the expressions.

1) What is another way to say this is a drag?_____

2) Is there another way to say get some shut eye?_____

3) How can you say that someone is considerably incorrect?_____

4) How can you say you've hit the limit?_____

5) What is another way to say you click?_____

■ **MAKE THIS MAKE SENSE:** Ask Student 2 to change these sentences to make sense.

1) We hit it off so famously that I hope we never see each other again.

2) I'm wide awake because I'm just about to snooze.

3) I'm just going through all my mail after my month-long vacation. It's no hassle at all.

4) Your credit card is good because you've maxed it out.

5) The politician's off-base comment won him the election.

Questions to Ask Someone from Student Group 3

Ask Student 3 the following questions. He or she will tell you the answers. You should write down the answers. Student 3 can look at pages 62-63 to find the answers.

■ **TELL ME:** Ask Student 3 following questions to get the expressions.

1) Is there a way to say that you feel thrilled about something?_____

2) How can you describe someone who knows what they're talking about?_____

3) What is a way to say a mistake or malfunction?_____

4) What is a way to say you can catch on to something quickly?_____

5) Is there another way to say this is simply the best?_____

■ **MAKE THIS MAKE SENSE:** Ask Student 3 to change these sentences to make sense.

1) Your panoramic view of the telephone wires just can't be beat!

2) That student is so tough to teach that he picks up everything quickly!

3) Pele wouldn't make a good sports commentator because he isn't very savvy about organized soccer.

4) Our new phone system has no glitches at all. That's why we have all these party lines.

5) I'm sure she won't flip if you give her that spectacular necklace for Valentine's Day.

Students 1—2—3

Before you begin the Halftime Activities, you must first complete pages 58-66. These activities are designed to get you to think about and discuss any extended meaning and use of the expressions you have just studied.

■ **EXPRESSION GUIDE:** With your classmates or with a native speaker, look at the Expression Guide below to find out if there is any information to add about the expressions. Write down anything interesting you discover. You can use some of the questions below to get started:

1. Do you use these expressions? Why or why not?

2. Are there any other meanings related to the expressions?

3. Is there any special way to say these expressions?

4. Do you know how these expressions may have originated?

EXPRESSION GUIDE

the bottom line	tacky	hold out	twist my arm	click *slang*
hassle	off base	snooze	max out *slang*	hit it off
glitch *slang*	savvy *slang*	pick up	can't be beat	flip (out) *slang*

■ **FIND OUT MORE:** Below is more information about the meanings of some of the expressions as well as a few grammar tips.

1) the bottom line—There are a few other expressions containing the word **bottom**. See if you can pick up the meanings by matching the expressions below.
   a) bottoms up   ___your last amount of money
   b) hit rock bottom   ___the choices remaining, usually unwanted
   c) bottom dollar   ___cheers
   d) the bottom of the barrel ___at the lowest point

Now, complete the example using some of the expressions with **bottom**:

I was really scraping _____ because I didn't have a choice. Sometimes when you _____, you have nowhere to go but up. Fortunately, you were there for me and helped me out a lot. So here's to you: _____!

2) hold out—**Hold** is highly idiomatic as a phrasal verb: hold out (for), hold on, hold off and hold/held up. Each expression contains some nuance of "wait." Look at the examples below and decide which **hold** phrase best describes the meaning of wait.

   a) I got another call. Wait a second._____

   b) I think you should wait to decide._____

   c) Sorry I'm late, but I got stuck in traffic._____

   d) I see. You think the grass is greener on the other side._____

Two other expressions containing a meaning of wait are **hold your horses**, which means don't be impatient and **don't hold your breath**, which means don't wait for something to happen because your expectations are unrealistic. One other very common use of **hold** is **hold the (noun)**, which means stop or omit. Match these expressions next to t he example which best describes them.

   e) I don't want any onions on my burger._____

   f) I already told you that we're going to go soon._____

   g) He's not going to apologize._____

3) off base—This expression comes from the game of baseball, and there are two other very common idioms which are related. Think of a baseball field and guess the meanings of the following sentences:

   a) I'll **touch base** with you later to see how you're doing and how much progress you've made. _____

   b) Are you sure we've **covered all the bases**? We'd better triple check just to make sure._____

4) hit it off—There are more than 40 expressions containing **hit**. It's worth a look in an idiom dictionary. Here are just ten of the more interesting ones:

   a) **hit it**—start or leave
   b) **hit it big**—make a lot of money, become very successful
   c) **hit on**—try to seduce someone
   d) **hit someone up for something**—ask to borrow something, usually pejorative
   e) **a hit**—a drag, a puff; something very popular, usually a song
   f) **hit the spot**—satisfy one's hunger.
   g) **hit**—rob or assassinate
   h) **hit the books**—study a lot
   i) **hit the jackpot**—win or get lucky
   j) **hit the sack**—go to bed

Use some of the expressions above in the following examples:

   a) Come on, let's _____. I don't like this place because there are too many people _____ each other.

   b) Wow, you really _____ when you _____ playing blackjack!

c) I've got to _____ early because I have to wake up and _____ again before my test.

d) What? You want _____ off my cigarette now too? What else are you going to _____?

5) **pick up**—The phrasal verb **pick up** is highly prolific and is worth a look in an idioms dictionary. In addition to the two meanings we've studied in this chapter (learn indirectly and attempt to meet people of the opposite sex), here are several more: 1) to buy or acquire something, (2) to pay a tab or bill, (3) to clean up, straighten up, tidy up, (4) to go and get/receive something, and (5) give someone a ride. As a noun, **pickup**, also has a couple of meanings: (1) a small truck, and (2) a person of the opposite sex who is easy to meet. Based on these definitions, read the examples below and decide which meaning applies.

a) Louis: What's the damage?
Sam: George **picked it up** this time! _____

b) Can I borrow your **pickup**? I'm moving this weekend. _____

c) Lillian: Where did you get that table? It's great!
Annette: I **picked it up** at a garage sale. Can you believe it? _____

d) If you know Spanish, you can **pick up** Portuguese easily. _____

e) She looks easy to **pick up**. I bet I can get her number within 5 minutes. _____

f) I have to go to the post office to **pick up** my package. _____

g) I need to **pick up** my house before they come over tonight. _____

h) Would you **pick me up** from the airport on Monday? _____

6) **flip**—This slang expression has a few more meanings. It's important to pay attention to the intonation patterns when this expression is used. For example, the intonation will be quite different for someone who **flips out** because they are angry as opposed to someone who is really excited about something. The intonation would also be different to describe someone who **flips out** and goes insane. Another expression, which means to either become very angry or go insane, is **flip one's lid**. In addition, some people make an obscene gesture if they are very angry or rude—they **flip someone off**, or **give someone the finger**. It's very important not to make this gesture or react to it!

There are also two idioms containing **flip**: you can **flip a coin** to decide something by calling out heads or tails, and someone can **do a flip-flop**, which means to do the opposite of what is expected. Read the examples below and decide the meanings and possible intonation patterns: positive, neutral, or emotional (surprised, angry).

a) I can't believe it! That guy just cut me off and had the nerve to **flip me off** too! _____

b) Poor Jay cracked under all the pressure and **flipped out**. He had a nervous breakdown. _____

c) OK, let's **flip a coin**. Heads I win, tails you win. _____

d) Cody did a complete **flip-flop**. He was going to major in business, but he chose art instead. _____

■ **READ** the following and discuss the probable meanings of the underlined expressions. Circle any key words or phrases that help you to understand the meaning(s). Be sure to work with a partner.

1) OK—I'm going to <u>level with</u> you since you asked me for my opinion. I'm sorry if it hurts your feelings, but <u>the bottom line</u> is that you can't keep <u>fooling yourself</u> into thinking that you can <u>keep up with</u> this lifestyle. You're way over your budget. All your credit cards are <u>maxed out</u>, and it is really <u>tacky</u> when you try to <u>pick up</u> the tab for everyone and you have to keep trying to pay with another credit card...

2) Hey Kevin. Sorry to <u>hassle</u> you again about this, but there still seems to be <u>a glitch</u> in our system because the <u>pickups</u> never arrive on time and everyone gets <u>held up</u>. We had a customer <u>flip out</u> on us and threaten to move his business elsewhere. Luckily I was able to <u>schmooze</u> him into changing his mind, but I don't think I'll get so lucky next time.

3) What? Hawaii again?! How many times do we have to go there? <u>Twist my arm</u>! I dare you to make me go there again and <u>hang out</u> on that awful North Shore and <u>snooze</u> on that soft sandy beach and swim in that warm turquoise ocean. Just force me to eat all that fresh pineapple, <u>munch</u> on those tasty shrimp, and sip on fresh coconut milk. Then I'll have to go hiking in the forest and <u>check out</u> all the wild orchids, Hawaiian white ginger, gardenias. Then I'll get so bored that I'll have to go scuba diving and hang out with all those playful garibaldi fish... OK. I believe I've <u>covered all the bases</u>. A vacation in Hawaii just <u>can't be beat</u>!

4) I wouldn't <u>hold your breath</u> if I were you. I don't think things are going to be in our favor <u>straight away</u>. We've presented a very solid and reasonable proposal, but the manager just isn't very <u>savvy</u> about taking business risks. He can't see <u>the forest for the trees</u>. The idea that you've got to spend money to make money just doesn't <u>click</u> with him. But let's not <u>give up</u>.

5) Do you think you could <u>pick me up</u> from the office later today? I'm not sure what time I'll finish though because my car is still <u>in the shop</u>. This is such <u>a hassle</u>. Can I <u>touch base</u> with you later this afternoon and <u>give you an update</u>?

6) Linda is going to <u>flip</u> when she sees that store I told you about! It's like a museum, full of gorgeous Asian art and furniture. Some of it is a little <u>tacky</u> though, but most of it is fantastic. I <u>picked up</u> this little chest there. I got <u>a great deal</u> too because I paid cash. I tell you this place <u>can't be beat</u>!

7) Carlos and Lisa have really <u>hit it off</u>. The funny thing is that they met in a sports bar, but they didn't <u>pick up</u> on each other. They were sitting next to each other at different tables and they both ordered their cheeseburgers the exact same way: medium rare, sharp cheddar with <u>the works</u> but <u>hold the</u> mayonnaise.

8) Jack has really <u>hit rock bottom</u> since he got <u>laid off</u>. We can't even <u>twist his arm</u> into shooting some pool with us. I went over to his house the other day because he never <u>picks up</u> when I call. It seems like he's been <u>hitting</u>

the bottle because there were beer bottles everywhere. It looked like he hadn't picked up anything for at least two months. He was just snoozing in front of the TV.

9) We are going to have to hold out for a better offer because the one they gave us doesn't fit our needs. Their figures are still off base and I'm not sure how, or if, we can explain it to them more clearly. We just may have to start the search again and seek out another vendor. I like the people at this company a lot, but we just don't seem to click when it comes to placing orders with them. I don't want to hassle with this anymore.

10) Children are capable of picking up two or three or even four languages during childhood. Even if they don't use one of the languages until they grow up, they can still pronounce it like a native speaker. If they lived in that country, they could pick it up really quickly because it would click in their long term memory. Let's face it, learning a language when you're a kid just can't be beat!

■ **EXPRESSION LOG:** (1) Choose any 15 expressions from this chapter to practice by writing original sentences, then (2) add two new expressions that you hear. Follow the New Expression Guide in Appendix A.

■ **Listen** for the key words written in the boxes and number them in the order they are said. Write down the corresponding expressions. There is one expression for each key word

_____ key words: **out of line, knowledgeable** expressions:
_____ key words: **a huge bother, acquire, exasperated** expressions:
_____ key words: **top of the line, defects** expressions:
_____ key words: **overload, drowsy** expressions:
_____ key words: **withstand, win us over** expressions:
_____ key words: **fit together, get along really well, wasting my time** expressions:
_____ key words: **no class, the fact of the matter** expressions

RULES: Roll the die and move ahead to the corresponding box. Use the expression as indicated. Total up the points you earn. The first person to reach 21 wins. Speak clearly. Grammar counts.

20. savvy	21. skip a turn	22. hold out	23. WILD DRAW	24. the bottom
statement question 2 points	☹	future 2 point	☺ your choice 5 points	line statement 3 points
19. can't be beat	18. FREE CHOICE	17. miss a turn	16. hassle	15. glitch
statement 2 points	☺ 2 points	☹	negative 2 points	affirmative, past 3 points
10. off base	11. WILD DRAW	12. click	13. lose a turn	14. pick up
information question 1 points	☺ your choice, 5 points	past 2 points	☹	command 1 point
9. lose a turn	8. max out	7. hit it off	6. flip out	5. FREE CHOICE
☹	polite request 4 points	statement 2 points	information question 3 points	☺ 1 point
START	1. tacky	2. snooze	3. skip a turn	4. twist my arm
	simple question 2 points	present perfect 3 points	☹	request 3 points

Keep Score

Name	Name	Name	Name

flip out

5

a klutz

phony

come up with

right up your alley

know the ropes

a rookie

picky

glued to

spin your wheels

cold turkey

red tape

sleazy

chip in

stick your neck out

grin and bear it

Student Group 1

Learn the meanings of the following five expressions by completing the exercises. Work with Student Group 1 or by yourself.

■ **GUESS** the meanings of the five expressions.

1) I broke another glass! I'm such a **klutz**!

2) The people at the start-your-own-business meeting were so **phony**.

3) If we're going to give Rie a surprise party, we'll have to **come up with** a clever way to keep it from her.

4) Melih can fix it. That's **right up his alley**!

5) Ask Peter. He **knows the ropes** around here.

■ **CHECK OUT** the definitions and examples of the expressions.

1) **a klutz**—someone who is clumsy, who bumps into things or breaks things.
   I'm turning into a klutz! I bruised myself again.

2) **phony**—fake, insincere, not honest or real.
   Don't give your money to that phony telemarketing company!

3) **come up with**—think of a solution, find an idea, elaborate.
   Hiro came up with a great way to expand the program without spending much money.

4) **right up your alley**—suitable, pertinent, appropriate for someone.
   Carla would love this political commentary—it's right up her alley.

5) **know/learn the ropes**—understand how an organization or community functions.
   I've been here for three years and I'm still learning the ropes.

■ **QUICK FIX**—Match the expressions to the words that are similar.

1) know-how   ____right up your alley

2) artificial   ____learn the ropes

3) awkward   ____phony

4) suggest   ____ a klutz

5) fitting   ____ come up with

◼ **CLOZE IT**—Use one of the above expressions to complete the sentences. Be sure to pay attention to any necessary grammatical changes.

1) John _____ a great way to finish the project!

2) All that guy does is brag about how smart he is, but he isn't. He's so _____!

3) You're going to love this new restaurant. It's _____.

4) I wouldn't give that crystal vase to Sue if I were you. She's a bit of _____.

5) You'll _____ around here. It just takes a little time.

◼ **SENSE OR NONSENSE**—With your classmates, discuss these sentences and decide if they do or don't make sense.

1) Madonna never seems to come up with any new ideas for her music. _____

2) Tiger Woods is a big klutz on the golf course. _____

3) Many people think the typical politician is very phony. _____

4) A CEO is usually someone who has learned the ropes. _____

5) If you're looking for good waves, Hawaii is right up your alley. _____

◼ **PLUG IT IN**—Use the expressions to replace the underlined words. Make sure to check your grammar. Check the Index/Glossary for words you may not know.

1) Henry was on the team that designed the systems, so he <u>knows all the ins and outs</u>.

2) That was the most <u>insincere</u> apology I've ever heard in my life! What do you really want?

3) This novel is <u>just your cup of tea</u>! You're going to flip when you read it!

4) I'm <u>all thumbs</u> today! I've just spilled coffee again!

5) How did you <u>discover how to make</u> that delicious sauce?

Student Group 2

Learn the meanings of the following five expressions by completing the exercises. Work with Student Group 2 or by yourself.

■ **GUESS** the meanings of the five expressions.

1) Even though I've been studying this language for years, I still feel like a rookie sometimes!

2) Bruce wouldn't have liked the concert because he is so picky about music.

3) Helena is glued to her Play Station. She won't stop until she wins.

4) Don't hold your breath! You're spinning your wheels if you wait for an answer.

5) Rosa gave up caffeine cold turkey.

■ **CHECK OUT** the definitions and examples of the expressions.

1) a rookie—a person who is new at something, someone with little experience.
Omar is still a rookie, but he's learning fast!

2) picky —difficult to please, very particular.
Julie is very picky when it comes to eggs. She won't eat them unless they've been poached for exactly three minutes.

3) glued to—pay a lot of attention to something without interruption.
That movie was great! We were glued to the screen!

4) spin one's wheels—work hard without seeing a result.
I've been spinning my wheels for days on this project but I haven't made any progress.

5) (go) cold turkey—quit or stop something suddenly and completely.
Keiko gave up smoking cold turkey. Now she chews nicotine gum.

■ **QUICK FIX**—Match the expressions to the words that are similar.

1) fixated   ____spin one's wheels

2) abandon   ____rookie

3) trainee   ____go cold turkey

4) in vain   ____picky

5) choosy   ____be glued to

■ **CLOZE IT**—Use one of the above expressions to complete the sentences. Be sure to pay attention to any necessary grammatical changes.

1) Look, don't _____! There's probably a glitch.

2) I couldn't sleep last night because I _____ my book.

3) The senior employees will help train the _____.

4) Glen _____ last summer. He hasn't had a beer since!

5) Don't be so _____! This isn't a gourmet restaurant you know.

■ **SENSE OR NONSENSE**—With your classmates, discuss these sentences and decide if they do or don't make sense.

1) Going cold turkey is usually a very big challenge._____

2) Most elected officials are rookies in their field._____

3) When you spin your wheels, it's easy to cut corners._____

4) Really picky people are fun to travel to foreign countries with._____

5) We were glued to the radio. His speech was full of food for thought._____

■ **PLUG IT IN**—Use the expressions to replace the underlined words. Make sure to check your grammar. Check the Index/Glossary for words you may not know.

1) Kyu is <u>the new kid on the block</u>. He's still learning the ropes!

2) Jose is very <u>particular</u> about his clothes. They have to be a certain style.

3) We are <u>going around in circles</u>. Let's take a break and get some air.

4) I <u>can't stop listening to</u> my new CD. I'm completely mesmerized by that music.

5) Chen used to be totally hooked on TV, but he <u>gave it up totally</u> when he moved.

Student Group 3

Learn the meanings of the following five expressions by completing the exercises. Work with Student Group 3 or by yourself.

■ **GUESS** the meanings of the five expressions.

1) You have to follow this procedure. There's no way around the **red tape**.

2) Look at this **sleazy** bar. Everyone seems drunk.

3) If everyone **chips in**, we can finish early!

4) Axel **stuck his neck out**, asked for a raise and got it!

5) I don't like these new rules, but I'm going to **grin and bear it**.

■ **CHECK OUT** the definitions and examples of the expressions.

1) **red tape**—time-consuming delays because of bureaucratic or office policy.
   There is a lot of red tape to go through. You have to fill out all these forms in triplicate.

2) **sleazy**—dirty, cheap in character, disdainful.
   We could only find a sleazy motel. All the others were booked solid.

3) **chip in**—contribute, help.
   All ten of us chipped in $5.00 for the baby gift, so we ended up with $50.00 to spend.

4) **stick one's neck out**—take a risk which may backfire.
   I'm not going to stick my neck out for you again. You're such a flake!

5) **grin and bear it**—handle a difficult situation the best way possible.
   Another two hours to go...just grin and bear it!

■ **QUICK FIX**—Match the expressions to the words that are similar.

1) scummy   _____stick one's neck out

2) established rules _____chip in

3) endure   _____sleazy

4) chance it   _____red tape

5) lend a hand   _____grin and bear it

■ **CLOZE IT**—Use one of the above expressions to complete the sentences. Be sure to pay attention to any necessary grammatical changes.

1) I wish I didn't have to take this class! But, I might as well just _____.

2) There's no way you can get out of paying the late fee. There's too much _____.

3) That movie was totally _____. My mom would hate it!

4) Sarah decided to _____ and complain about the working conditions.

5) Thanks for _____. I couldn't have done it without you!

■ **SENSE OR NONSENSE**—With your classmates, discuss these sentences and decide if they do or don't make sense.

1) I hope he takes me to a sleazy restaurant for my birthday._____

2) Going through all the red tape takes no time at all!_____

3) For the potluck party, Mara brought fondue, Yoshi brought sushi, Emir brought ice cream, and I chipped in with the beverages._____

4) Olympic athletes should grin and bear it if they lose._____

5) To become successful in business, you never have to stick your neck out._____

■ **PLUG IT IN**—Use the expressions to replace the underlined words. Make sure to check your grammar. Check the Index/Glossary for words you may not know.

1) That guy is <u>contemptible</u>. I don't trust him at all.

2) The neighbors <u>supplied</u> most of the camping equipment for all the children.

3) I <u>put myself in a vulnerable position</u> when I told it to him straight.

4) The weather is terrible again! We'll have to <u>put up with staying</u> at home again.

5) The government <u>bureaucracy</u> costs taxpayers a lot of money!

Questions to Ask Someone from Student Group 1

Ask Student 1 the following questions. He or she will tell you the answers. You should write down the answers. Student 1 can look at pages 76-77 to find the answers.

■ **TELL ME:** Ask Student 1 the following questions to get the expressions.

1) What do you call someone who breaks or drops things a lot?_____

2) How can you say something was made just for you?_____

3) What's another word for superficial or fake?_____

4) Is there a way to say you understand all the details about a place?_____

5) What is another way to say think of or imagine?_____

■ **MAKE THIS MAKE SENSE:** Ask Student 1 to change these sentences to make sense.

1) Governors can become presidents if they don't learn the ropes of the federal government.

2) Einstein never came up with any original ideas regarding light, time, and space.

3) I'm sure this is the bottom-line price because the salesperson seemed so phony.

4) If you love hot weather, then living in Alaska would be right up your alley.

5) A prima ballerina has to be a klutz.

Questions to Ask Someone from Student Group 2

Ask Student 2 the following questions. He or she will tell you the answers. You should write down the answers. Student 2 can look at pages 78-79 to find the answers.

■ **TELL ME:** Ask Student 2 the following questions to get the expressions.

1) What is a way to say you've quit something completely?_____

2) Is there another expression that means to be hooked on?_____

3) What can you call someone who is a novice?_____

4) How can you describe someone who likes things a certain way?_____

5) What is a way to say you're working hard but not seeing any progress?_____

■ **MAKE THIS MAKE SENSE:** Ask Student 2 to change these sentences to make sense.

1) We were so glued to the movie that we fell asleep.

2) A very picky person will usually try any kind of food.

3) Three-step programs are designed to help you stop smoking cold turkey.

4) Promoting the rookie to manager would be a great idea.

5) Spinning your wheels gives you a very satisfying feeling of accomplishment.

Questions to Ask Someone from Student Group 3

Ask Student 3 the following questions. He or she will tell you the answers. You should write down the answers. Student 3 can look at pages 80-81 to find the answers.

■ **TELL ME:** Ask Student 3 following questions to get the expressions.

1) Is there a way to describe something that doesn't look very reputable?_____

2) How can you tell someone to take a courageous chance?_____

3) What is a way to say to make the best out of a bad situation?_____

4) Is there an expression to describe lots of inflexible procedures?_____

5) What's another way to say lend a hand?_____

■ **MAKE THIS MAKE SENSE:** Ask Student 3 to change these sentences to make sense.

1) You can always count on flaky people to chip in.

2) We stayed in a five-star hotel. It was totally sleazy.

3) Nelson Mandela couldn't grin and bear it for those dozens of years in prison. That's just one reason why he became the President of South Africa.

4) A red-tape procedure is a piece of cake.

5) Political candidates can't stick their necks out if they want to get elected.

Students 1—2—3

Before you begin the Halftime Activities, you must first complete pages 76-84. These activities are designed to get you to think about and discuss any extended meaning and use of the expressions you have just studied.

■ **EXPRESSION GUIDE:** With your classmates or with a native speaker, look at the Expression Guide below to find out if there is any information to add about the expressions. Write down anything interesting you discover. You can use some of the questions below to get started:

1. Do you use these expressions? Why or why not?

2. Are there any other meanings related to the expressions?

3. Is there any special way to say these expressions?

4. Do you know how these expressions may have originated?

EXPRESSION GUIDE

a klutz *slang*	phony	come up with	right up your alley	know the ropes
a rookie *slang*	picky	be glued to	spin your wheels	cold turkey
red tape	sleazy	chip in	stick your neck out	grin and bear it

■ **FIND OUT MORE:** Below is more information about the meanings of some of the expressions as well as a few grammar tips.

1) **come up with**—There are many frequently used phrasal verb expressions containing the verb **come**. For example, **come up** means that something happens unexpectedly. **Come off** is an expression which describes the effect or impression of something or someone. **Come off it** means to stop trying to

pretend that something is real or true. **Come across** is similar in meaning to **come off** because it also means to give an impression, but it also means to find or discover something by chance. You've probably heard of **come on**, which means please or hurry up. Did you know it also means to stop joking around? There is also a slang expression **come on (to)** someone, which means to make sexual advances or flirt heavily. Look at the examples below, choose the best expression to complete the thoughts, then describe the meaning.

Examples: **Meaning:**

a) _____, we're going to be late!   _____

b) I _____ a great antique   _____
store last Saturday. It's really funky!

c) Can you believe the way that guy _____?   _____
He thinks he's Don Juan!

d) Oh! _____! That's absurd.   _____

e) Colin was trying to play it cool, but he _____   _____
_____like a bozo.

2) **right up your alley**—Here are six more expressions with the word **right**. See if you can match them to the corresponding words on the right:

a) I'd **give my right arm** to have that opportunity!   ___**1)** conservative

b) I just knew he was **Mr. Right**.   ___**2)** to the point
It was my gut feeling.

c) We walked into this shop and, **right off the bat**, the ___**3)** the best mate
salesguy told us he'd cut us the best deal in town.

d) Republicans tend to be **right-wing** or conventional   ___**4)** immediately
while Democrats tend to be left-wing or liberal.

e) That speech was **right on the money**. It's exactly   ___**5)** great
what people are thinking!   correct

f) We'll meet you after the game then. **Right on!**   ___**6)** envy, be ready
That'll work out fine.   to sacrifice

3) **spin your wheels**—There are a few more expressions containing the word **spin**. Read the examples below and write a definition for the underlined expressions.

a) It's a gorgeous day. How about going for **a spin**?

_____

b) The car hit the ice and **spun out** of control.

_____

c) Everything happened so fast that it **made my head spin**.

_____

d) That radio talk show host is always **putting his spin** on whatever any-one else says. He thinks he's a **spin doctor**!

_____

4) **cold turkey**—**Cold** is used in a few more popular expressions. If someone **gives you the cold shoulder**, they treat you in a very impersonal way or ignore you. If you get **cold feet**, you're too scared to do something difficult.

If someone murders someone **in cold blood**, they are completely ruthless. Of course, most of us have heard of the **Cold War** between the former Soviet Union and the United States. Look at the sentences below and complete them using the best expression containing **cold**.

a) A lot of high technology came out of the espionage during the _____.

b) The murderer killed his wife _____.

c) The film *Runaway Bride* is about a woman who gets _____ because she isn't sure she has met Mr. Right.

d) We had a little disagreement a year ago, but my neighbor still gives me the _____.

5) red tape—**Red** is another word that is used in some interesting expressions. See if you can find the expressions that best fit the following underlined descriptions:

a) Whenever the president travels anywhere, he gets <u>the royal treatment</u>!

___**1) the red-eye**

b) The employees all worked overtime, but they <u>didn't get any more money</u>!

___**2) roll out the red carpet**

c) I'm going to take <u>a late flight</u> to New York. I hope I won't feel too tired in the morning!

___**3) a redneck**

d) Billy won't hire anyone who isn't white. His <u>mentality is really limited</u>!

___**4) not a red cent**

6) chip in—Following are three classic idioms containing the word **chip**. Read the examples and write definitions for the underlined expressions.

a) He looks, thinks and acts so much like his dad. He really is **a chip off the old block**.

You can tell he is his father's son!

_____

b) Scott really has **a chip on his shoulder**. Whenever he feels the least bit insecure, he is ready to attack.

_____

c) When **the chips are down**, in a traditional marriage, you stay together no matter what.

_____

7) stick your neck out—**Stick** is another highly idiomatic word. Check out the sentences below to see if you can match the corresponding expressions:

stick up for   sticky   the sticks   stick out like a sore thumb

a) If you dye your hair lime green, you'll _____.

b) I come from a really small town, so you wouldn't know the name. It's out in _____.

c) This is a very _____ situation. We'd better handle it carefully.

d) The workers decided to _____ their rights, so they went on strike.

■ **READ** the following and discuss the probable meanings of the underlined expressions. Circle any key words or phrases that help you to understand the meaning(s). Be sure to work with a partner.

1) I was <u>channel surfing</u> the other night and <u>came across</u> a fabulous series on TV called *The Sopranos*. Since then, I've been <u>glued to</u> my TV whenever it's on. I know how <u>picky</u> you are when it comes to TV shows, but believe me, it's the type of show that's <u>right up your alley</u>!

2) Kevin has had plenty of experience <u>dealing with</u> all the <u>red tape</u> of the university. He <u>learned the ropes</u> quite awhile ago, so he knows who to <u>hook up with</u> so that you don't <u>spin your wheels</u> with all the paperwork that has to be processed.

3) I know I'm a <u>rookie</u> around here, but I'm going to <u>stick my neck out</u> and give the boss a few <u>tips</u>. I hope I don't <u>come off</u> as being arrogant, but I'm certain that we can <u>cut some corners</u> and get the job done faster and more efficiently.

4) Our car <u>broke down</u> in the middle of nowhere, and our cell phone didn't work, so we had to wait for someone to drive by us and give us <u>a lift</u> to the nearest gas station. Finally a truck driver <u>picked us up</u> and took us to a gas station that had a <u>redneck</u> mechanic who kept making <u>wisecracks</u> about foreign cars. We had to grin and bear it for two days in a <u>sleazy</u> motel waiting for the car part to arrive. We were really in <u>the sticks</u>.

5) I wish I could <u>come up with</u> a more exciting story about how I got this magnificent bruise on my leg, but the fact is that I was walking! That's right. Walking! I wasn't biking, skiing, playing tennis, or anything of the sort. We decided to go for <u>a spin</u> because it was such a clear day. I got out of the car to take a picture, and BOOM! <u>Right off the bat,</u> I fell down! What <u>a klutz</u>!

6) I'm sorry, <u>buddy</u>, but I can't <u>stick up for</u> you anymore. You've got too much of <u>a chip on your shoulder</u>. I'm not going to be <u>phony</u> with you and <u>take your side</u> every time you get <u>rubbed the wrong way</u>. I'm going to be a <u>real</u> friend to you and <u>tell it to you straight</u>: You've got to <u>take a long hard look</u> at yourself and <u>figure out</u> why you react the way you do.

7) If you take the <u>red-eye</u> here to spend the long weekend, believe me, we'll <u>roll out the red carpet</u> for you! We'll even <u>chip in</u> for your flight! Now <u>come on</u>! You've got to be here for this surprise party! Don't get <u>cold feet</u>! Just come! It's easy! Just get on the plane, OK?

8) I knew he wasn't <u>Mr. Right</u> because of the way he <u>came on to me</u> the second time we went out after work. And <u>on top of that</u>, he was always <u>putting his ultra-right-wing spin</u> on everything, especially when he was telling me about how to vote. I'm going to have to give him the <u>cold shoulder</u> next time I <u>run into</u> him. This could be a little <u>sticky</u> because we are doing a project together, but I'll <u>grin and bear it</u>.

9) I would <u>give my right arm</u> to be able to go <u>cold turkey</u> and quit smoking the way you did! You should be really proud of yourself not <u>to be hooked on</u>

cigarettes anymore. I know it felt like your <u>head was spinning</u> for a while because you were so used to smoking, but you <u>stuck it out</u>. <u>Right on</u>! <u>Way to go</u>!

10) Whenever it rains, Brian loves taking that old beat-up <u>pick-up</u>, which isn't worth <u>a red cent</u>, out for <u>a spin</u> in the rain and he doesn't mind <u>sticking out like a sore thumb</u> driving through town afterward caked in mud. Like his two older brothers, he is <u>a chip off the old block</u>. I believe that truck will stay in the family for years to come.

■ **EXPRESSION LOG:** (1) Choose any 15 expressions from this chapter to practice by writing original sentences, then (2) add two new expressions that you hear. Follow the New Expression Guide in Appendix A.

- Listen to the questions and choose an expression(s) to use in your answer.
- Listen to the questions again and write a complete response using the expression.
- You will have one minute to write each sentence.

picky	chip in	learn/know the ropes	phony	be glued to
grin and bear it	a rookie	sleazy	sticky	stick your neck out
right up your alley	cold turkey	a spin	come up with	a klutz
red tape	spin your wheels	come off it	right on	the sticks
cold shoulder	come on	right-winged	chip off the old block	redneck

Expression	Response
1.	
2.	
3.	
4.	
5.	
6.	
7.	
8.	
9.	
10.	

RULES: Double Dice.
- Roll the die and go to the corresponding box.
- Roll the die again. If the number is:
- ODD (1,3,5) use the expression in an upbeat or sarcastic tone.
- EVEN (2,4,6) use the expression in a neutral or disappointed tone.
- Go around the board at least two times. Mark your place by writing your names.

s) come off it	r) cold war	q) redneck	p) right on (the money)	o) cold turkey
Names _____ _____ _____	**Names** _____ _____ _____	**Names** _____ _____ _____	**Names** _____ _____ _____	**Names** _____ _____ _____
j) right up your alley	k) come up with	l) a klutz	m) spin your wheels	n) learn/know the ropes
Names _____ _____ _____	**Names** _____ _____ _____	**Names** _____ _____ _____	**Names** _____ _____ _____	**Names** _____ _____ _____
i) picky	h) grin and bear it	g) chip in	f) sleazy	e) red tape
Names _____ _____ _____	**Names** _____ _____ _____	**Names** _____ _____ _____	**Names** _____ _____ _____	**Names** _____ _____ _____
Start	a) phony	b) be glued to	c) stick your neck out	d) a rookie
	Names _____ _____ _____	**Names** _____ _____ _____	**Names** _____ _____ _____	**Names** _____ _____ _____

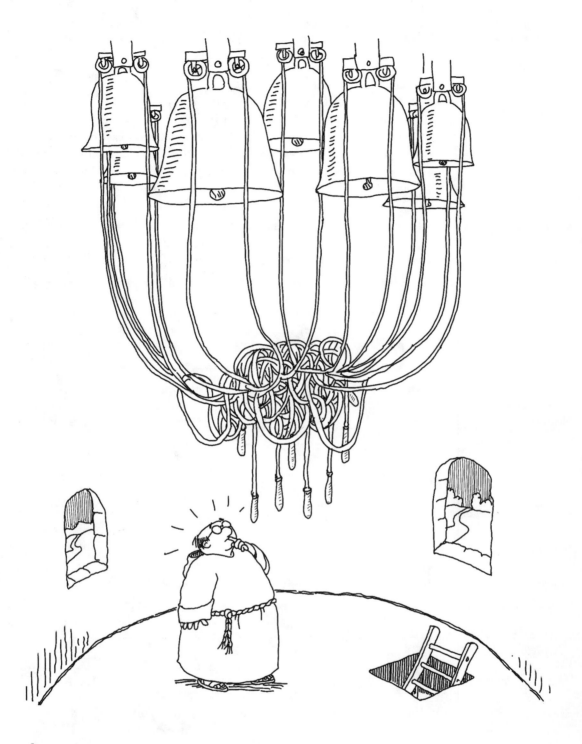

know the ropes

6

a tough act to follow

Student Group 1

Learn the meanings of the following five expressions by completing the exercises. Work with Student Group 1 or by yourself.

■ **GUESS** the meanings of the five expressions.

1) David is a great employee. You can **count on** him to get the job done.

2) I **heard through the grapevine** that you're thinking about buying a new Harley Davidson.

3) That was a **decent** steak. Not too bad at all.

4) Neither of us had gone scuba diving before, so we decided to **give it a shot** while we were on vacation in the Bahamas.

5) I don't know how I found this place. I just followed my **hunch**.

■ **CHECK OUT** the definitions and examples of the expressions.

1) **count on**—depend on, rely on, believe in.
   If I have a problem, I know I can count on my mom to help me out.

2) **through the grapevine**—information (often secret) spread by word of mouth.
   Rolf told me he found out about Jim's promotion through the grapevine.

3) **decent**—acceptable, standard.
   We thought the movie was decent, but I'd wait until it comes out on video.

4) **give something a shot**—try or attempt something.
   Henrik isn't much of a fish person, but I talked him into giving the Maine lobster a shot.

5) **a hunch**—perception, intuition.
   Come on, let's follow our hunch and pick some numbers—the lotto is up to $60 million!

■ **QUICK FIX**—Match the expressions to the words that are similar.

1) all right   _____give something a shot

2) gut feeling   _____hear through the grapevine

3) trust   _____a hunch

4) go for it   _____decent

5) rumor   _____count on

■ **CLOZE IT**—Use one of the above expressions to complete the sentences. Be sure to pay attention to any necessary grammatical changes.

1) Oh no, I locked my keys in my car! It's a good thing I can _____ the Auto Club to help me out.

2) Emiko said she had _____ that we should leave sooner. She was right!

3) We stayed in a _____ hotel, but it's nothing to write home about.

4) Rachael _____ that he wants to ask you out!

5) Tae-Eun decided to _____ snowboarding _____. Now she'd rather snowboard than ski!

■ **SENSE OR NONSENSE**—With your classmates, discuss these sentences and decide if they do or don't make sense.

1) Drivers need a car they can count on._____

2) You can always believe whatever you hear through the grapevine._____

3) It's good to follow your hunch._____

4) The weather in Southern California is pretty decent during winter._____

5) Gutless people love to give new things a shot._____

■ **PLUG IT IN**—Use the expressions to replace the underlined words. Make sure to check your grammar. Check the Index/Glossary for words you may not know.

1) Mathilde had <u>a premonition</u> that this was going to happen.

2) I didn't hear the news directly. I found out <u>in a roundabout way</u>.

3) Ahmed is a good guy. You can <u>bank on</u> him for sound advice.

4) Fernando loves working with wood, so he's going to <u>venture into wood carving</u>.

5) My boss and I had a <u>respectable</u> discussion about the office problems.

Student Group 2

Learn the meanings of the following five expressions by completing the exercises. Work with Student Group 2 or by yourself.

■ **GUESS** the meanings of the five expressions.

1) My neighbor is **on my case** about trimming my fruit trees. He says the fruit falls all over his backyard.

2) I'm lucky with all the driving I do. I haven't had a speeding ticket for three years. I'd better **knock on wood**!

3) Juliana **called off** the wedding at the last minute with no explanation! Rick was devastated.

4) The presidential candidates are **playing hardball** with all the negative campaigning.

5) You're going to work out at the gym again today? You really are **a glutton for punishment**.

■ **CHECK OUT** the definitions and examples of the expressions.

1) **on someone's case**—put pressure on or criticize someone about something. *The doctor is on my case about changing my eating habits because my blood pressure is too high.*

2) **knock on wood**—a gesture or expression used to prevent bad luck. *I haven't been sick for three years. I better knock on wood!*

3) **call off**—cancel an event. *The game was called off because of the rain, so we got a rain check.*

4) **play hardball**—aggressive or tough competition. *The construction companies are going to play hardball in order to get the bid to build the new ballpark.*

5) **glutton for punishment**—someone who does or wants something unpleasant. *Craig is a glutton for punishment. He does his own cooking, cleaning, and laundry.*

■ **QUICK FIX**—Match the expressions to the words that are similar.

1) ruthless   _____call off

2) greedy   _____play hardball

3) protect   _____on someone's case

4) stop _____glutton for punishment

5) bug someone _____knock on wood

■ **CLOZE IT**—Use one of the above expressions to complete the sentences. Be sure to pay attention to any necessary grammatical changes.

1) The meeting _____ because the time was inconvenient.

2) My teacher _____ about coming to class late.

3) He goes to bed late and wakes up early. He's _____.

4) My boyfriend and I haven't ever had a fight. _____!

5) Many people aren't cut out for sales because they have to _____.

■ **SENSE OR NONSENSE**—With your classmates, discuss these sentences and decide if they do or don't make sense.

1) I've never broken a bone. Knock on wood._____

2) Schmoozers always play hardball._____

3) People don't usually mind if you call off Saturday night plans at the last minute._____

4) Parents should never get on their children's case about homework._____

5) We're going to work this whole weekend. We're such gluttons for punishment._____

■ **PLUG IT IN**—Use the expressions to replace the underlined words. Make sure to check your grammar. Check the Index/Glossary for words you may not know.

1) Lisa postponed her party because so many people couldn't make it.

2) Jodi has been bugging her husband about his gambling habit.

3) You'd better cover every corner of this contract because they're not going to cut you any slack.

4) Leon is a workaholic. He burns the candle at both ends every single day and every single night!

5) You'd better count your lucky stars you haven't had an accident!

Student Group 3

Learn the meanings of the following five expressions by completing the exercises. Work with Student Group 3 or by yourself.

■ **GUESS** the meanings of the five expressions.

1) We'll be hard pressed to find someone to replace Betty because she's **a tough act to follow**. She doesn't miss a beat!

2) Before you leave your job, make sure you have something to **fall back on**.

3) Whatever scandal he's connected to, he always **comes out smelling like a rose**.

4) You need to **lighten up**. Take a break and relax a bit!

5) **Crooked** companies typically make offers that seem too good to be true.

■ **CHECK OUT** the definitions and examples of the expressions.

1) **a tough act to follow**—someone whose performance is so outstanding that it will be difficult to find someone else as good.
   The concert was great! The first band was a tough act to follow. Everyone booed the second band.

2) **fall back on**—have an alternative plan for protection in case of failure.
   Bob was lucky he could fall back on his parents after his company went bankrupt.

3) **come out smelling like a rose**—have a favorable outcome after a suspicious situation.
   She came out smelling like a rose in spite of all the rumors.

4) **lighten up**—relax, not take things too seriously or personally.
   Everyone is under the gun to finish the project, so lighten up. We're all in the same boat.

5) **crooked**—not on the level, untrustworthy, illegal.
   The cop was crooked. He accepted the bribe from the drug dealers.

■ **QUICK FIX**—Match the expressions to the words that are similar.

1) take it easy   _____crooked

2) take someone's place   _____lighten up

3) not legitimate   _____fall back on

4) rely on   _____come out smelling like a rose

5) shine through   _____a tough act to follow

■ **CLOZE IT**—Use one of the above expressions to complete the sentences. Be sure to pay attention to any necessary grammatical changes.

1) While Tammy was putting herself through law school, she knew she could always _____ the family business if she couldn't pass the bar.

2) Helen had better _____ or else she's going to make everyone feel uptight.

3) The Clintons always seem to _____ no matter what controversies they have been associated with.

4) I had a hunch this offer was _____. It just didn't add up.

5) Cristine was such _____ that it took two years to find someone to take her place.

■ **SENSE OR NONSENSE**—With your classmates, discuss these sentences and decide if they do or don't make sense.

1) Mohandas Gandhi was a tough act to follow._____

2) The comedian Eddie Murphy needs to lighten up._____

3) The government should provide people with something to fall back on._____

4) Some politicians have crooked reputations._____

5) The criminal was found innocent. He has come out smelling like a rose._____

■ **PLUG IT IN**—Use the expressions to replace the underlined words. Make sure to check your grammar. Check the Index/Glossary for words you may not know.

1) Despite the scandals of the Kennedy presidency, JFK <u>is still a beloved American president</u>.

2) If all else fails, I can always <u>return to</u> my old job.

3) They got caught because of their <u>fraudulent</u> scheme, so now they're doing time.

4) June never remarried because her husband was <u>irreplaceable</u>.

5) Scott should <u>chill out</u> and change his snotty attitude.

Questions to Ask Someone from Student Group 1

Ask Student 1 the following questions. He or she will tell you the answers. You should write down the answers. Student 1 can look at pages 94-95 to find the answers.

■ **TELL ME:** Ask Student 1 the following questions to get the expressions.

1) What is a way to say you heard about something through gossip?_____

2) Is there another expression for a gut feeling?_____

3) How can you tell someone to try something?_____

4) What is a way to describe something that is good enough?_____

5) Is there a way to say you can confide in or rely on someone?_____

■ **MAKE THIS MAKE SENSE:** Ask Student 1 to change these sentences to make sense.

1) It's sound advice to make important decisions based on what you hear through the grapevine.

2) If you're afraid of water, you should give windsurfing a shot.

3) People in countries torn apart by civil war can count on their neighbors to help them out.

4) Tyrannical dictators are decent leaders. That's why so many people fear them.

5) Logical people always follow their hunches.

Questions to Ask Someone from Student Group 2

Ask Student 2 the following questions. He or she will tell you the answers. You should write down the answers. Student 2 can look at pages 96-97 to find the answers.

■ **TELL ME:** Ask Student 2 the following questions to get the expressions.

1) What is a way to describe fierce competition?_____

2) What can you say to protect yourself from bad luck?_____

3) If someone is bugging you about something, they are_____

4) What can you call someone who overdoes it?_____

5) What is an expression that means to cancel?_____

■ **MAKE THIS MAKE SENSE:** Ask Student 2 to change these sentences to make sense.

1) It's really fun for the audience when a concert is called off.

2) If you're a glutton for punishment, you lead a balanced life.

3) I love to work for a boss who is always on my case about something.

4) If you want something bad to happen, you'd better knock on wood.

5) Trial lawyers don't have to play hardball when they're trying to win their case.

Questions to Ask Someone from Student Group 3

Ask Student 3 the following questions. He or she will tell you the answers. You should write down the answers. Student 3 can look at pages 98-99 to find the answers.

■ **TELL ME:** Ask Student 3 following questions to get the expressions.

1) What's another way to say calm down?_____

2) Is there another way to describe someone who isn't on the level?_____

3) How can you describe someone who always leaves a good impression no matter what they do?_____

4) Is there an expression to describe someone who is difficult to replace?_____

5) What is a way to say you have an alternative plan in case you need it?_____

■ **MAKE THIS MAKE SENSE:** Ask Student 3 to change these sentences to make sense.

1) Richard Nixon, the only U.S. president forced to resign, came out smelling like a rose after the Watergate Scandal.

2) You can have a strong sense of security if you have nothing to fall back on.

3) If you learn to lighten up, your blood pressure will increase a lot.

4) Crooked people make great business partners.

5) One reason Madonna became famous is that she wasn't a tough act to follow.

Students 1−2−3

Before you start the Halftime Activities, you must first complete pages 94-102. These activities are designed to get you to think about and discuss any extended meaning and use of the expressions you have just studied.

■ **EXPRESSION GUIDE:** With your classmates or with a native speaker, look at the Expression Guide below to find out if there is any information to add about the expressions. Write down anything interesting you discover. You can use some of the questions below to get started:

1. Do you use these expressions? Why or why not?

2. Are there any other meanings related to the expressions?

3. Is there any special way to say these expressions?

4. Do you know how these expressions may have originated?

EXPRESSION GUIDE

count on	through the grapevine	decent *slang*	give something a shot	a hunch
on someone's case *slang*	knock on wood	call off	play hardball	glutton for punishment
a tough act to follow	fall back on	come out smelling like a rose	lighten up *slang*	crooked

■ **FIND OUT MORE:** Below is more information about the meanings of some of the expressions as well as a few grammar tips.

1) count on— The phrasal verb **count on** means to rely on, but what do you think **count out** or **count in** means? How about **count off** or **countdown**? Can you guess what **don't count your chickens before they hatch** means? Check out the examples below and select the best corresponding description.

a) If you guys are going to play football, you can **count me out**. It's raining!

___number to make a group

b) You're getting married in ten days? Time for the **countdown**!

___exclude me

c) The teacher **counted off** in threes to make four groups from 12 students.

___include me

d) It's snowing—great! **Count me in** if you're going skiing this weekend!

___be overconfident about getting something

e) You're going to buy a new car because you think you're getting a bonus? **Don't count your chickens before they hatch!**

___the final moments

2) **give something a shot**—**Shot** is a word that is used in many colorful expressions. If you drink too many **shots** of tequila and feel drunk, your thinking might be **off by a long shot**. If you're **calling the shots**, your decisions won't be a **shot in the dark**. Did you know that Las Vegas is famous for **shotgun** weddings? Las Vegas also has a lot of **big shot** gamblers. Read the examples below and write definitions for the underlined expressions containing **shot**.

a) When you choose your lottery numbers, you're really taking **a shot in the dark**.

_____

b) They had **a shotgun wedding** in May and had a baby in June!

_____

c) If you order an oyster **shot**, you have to swallow it all at once.

_____

d) When he asked me how many words there are in the English language, I thought there were about 200,000. Actually there are over 600,000. I was **off by a long shot**!

_____

e) Who **calls the shots** in your family? Your mom or your dad? Or both? Or you?

_____

f) That guy in the limousine must be some kind of **a big shot**.

_____

3) **on someone's case**—If someone is (a) **on your case**, soon you hope that he or she will be (b) **off your case**; otherwise, you may go crazy and become a (c) **basketcase**. If that happens, you may have (d) **a case** to take to court. (e) **A case in point** is all the harassment lawsuits awaiting trial. Match the expressions to their definitions below.

___legal paperwork ___an example ___bug ___stop bothering ___stressed out

4) **knock on wood**—Here are a few more interesting expressions containing the word **knock**. Read the examples and match them to their definitions.

a) You'd better **knock it off**, or I'm going to get upset!

___renders unconscious

b) Mike Tyson usually **knocks out** his opponents.

___help yourself; do what you want

c) Many people think Cindy Crawford is **a knockout**.

___can't complain

d) You want more ice cream? Go ahead, **knock yourself out**!

___stop it; cut it out

e) He had a terrible accident, but his nurse became his wife. **Can't knock that!**

___learn lessons through living

f) Joey went to the **school of hard knocks**. He won't make the same mistake twice.

___gorgeous

5) **call off**—Here are a few more common expressions containing the word **call**. **Call it a day**, **call it a night**, and **call it quits** all have the meaning of stop, similar to **call off**, but they don't mean to cancel. If someone tells you that **you missed your calling**, it means you should be in a different line of work. If someone **calls your bluff**, they know you are cheating or trying to do something that isn't right. Another similar expression is to **call someone on something**, which means you know that someone is claiming to know or do something that isn't real. Also, don't forget what **call the shots** means! Use an expression to complete the sentences below.

a) You should have been an actor, not a teacher! You really _____.

b) I've been here since 7:15 a.m. Time to _____ It's almost dark already!

c) He said he could speak French, but I _____ He didn't even understand "out."

d) I won $300.00 in the poker game because no one _____.

e) Most people think the director _____, but it's really the assistant director who makes the decisions.

6) **play hardball**—There are lots of funny expressions with the words **play** and **hard**. In fact, do you know what it means to **play hard**? How about **play hard-to-get**? Have you ever **played doctor** or **played dumb**? Do you **play the game** at work? Are you the type who **plays around**? And did you ever get caught and **learn the hard way**? Choose the expressions which best fit the examples below and write brief definitions.

a) Men love challenges. That's why typical male behavior is to chase the women who never seem to be interested in going out with them. She's the one who _____.

_____

b) Ronald learned the ropes quickly and got several promotions, but now he has to _____ and schmooze to get ahead.

_____

c) Romeo _____ on his girlfriend again, so she dumped him. Now he's been begging her to come back, but she won't because he disgusts her. Maybe he _____, and the next girl he falls for he'll treat better.

_____

d) We really _____ on our vacation! It was so much fun. We went waterskiing and scuba diving. We also played some tennis. And we saw two concerts and three movies. It's was a blast!

_____

e) When your mom asked me if I knew where you were, I _____ because I didn't want you to get in trouble. But this is the last time I cover for you.

_____

f) OK, you _____ and I'll play nurse. No, I'll _____ and you play patient.

_____

7) **a tough act to follow**—Here are a few more common idioms with **act**. If someone tells you to **clean up your act**, you'd better **get your act together** and straighten yourself out. If your car starts **acting up**, you'd better take it to the mechanic. If your kids start **acting up**, you'd better straighten them out. If someone starts to **act out**, maybe they are upset about something. If someone starts to **act all high and mighty**, they probably think they are better than you. Read the following examples and match them to the definitions.

a) My sinus is **acting up**. I better get some medicine.

___arrogant, look down on others

b) Vera really **has her act together**. She takes care of her family and she runs a successful business.

___becoming irritated or not functioning

c) Harry had better **clean up his act** and study harder if he wants to pass the class.

___be organized and in control

d) Little Daniel is **acting out** against his mom because his dad is never home.

___behave better

e) Sometimes rich people **act all high and mighty** because they think their money makes them superior to others.

___react negatively

■ **READ** the following and discuss the probable meanings of the underlined expressions. Circle any key words or phrases that help you to understand the meaning(s). Be sure to work with a partner.

1) We had a <u>decent</u> weekend even though our ski trip got <u>called off</u>. We didn't do anything special, just sort of <u>hung out</u>, <u>played around</u> on the computer, <u>caught a couple of flicks</u>, and <u>kicked back</u> at home. <u>Can't knock that</u>!

2) They wanted to <u>play hardball</u> with new clients to <u>knock them down</u> on their price, so I <u>played the game</u> for awhile. But then it got to the point where it was obvious that we had to <u>lighten up</u>, or else we would <u>push them away</u>. They would <u>end up</u> thinking we were just plain greedy to the point of being <u>crooked</u>.

3) My little brother always <u>comes out smelling like a rose</u> in my mother's eyes no matter what he does. He can <u>get away with almost anything</u>. <u>Case in point</u>: the time he accidentally spilled grape juice on her brand new carpet. He somehow managed to fabricate this elaborate story about how a violent gust of wind blew in some rotten plums from our prolific tree just as he was waking up. Of course he didn't see them and just stepped on them and ground them into the carpet. She <u>fell for it</u>. He really <u>missed his calling</u>. He should have been a lawyer, not a caterer.

4) Juan has two part-time jobs, goes to school, and works out in the gym almost every day. He's really <u>gotten it together</u> since he <u>cleaned up his act</u> and decided to focus on his future. He used to be <u>a real glutton for punishment</u> by partying almost every night. His girlfriend was always <u>on his case</u> about that. But he <u>straightened up</u> because he realized that you can't <u>count on</u> anyone else to make you change; you have to do it yourself.

5) Marie told me she has learned to follow her <u>hunch</u> because every time she didn't, she had to <u>learn the hard way</u>. She got tired of going to <u>the school of hard knocks</u>, so she <u>wised up</u>, quit caring so much about what other people think, and <u>gave her gut feelings a shot</u>.

6) We heard <u>through the grapevine</u> that you're thinking about organizing another camping trip to the desert in spring. We're going to <u>twist your arm</u> into letting us <u>pitch in</u>. Last year's trip to Catalina Island will sure <u>be a tough act to follow</u>. It was great to get everyone together for that! You can definitely <u>count us in</u> for this trip. Let's just <u>knock on wood</u> that the weather will be as good as it was last year. If it's not, we can always <u>hang out</u> at George's beach cottage.

7) Ever since Brendon got his bonus, he's been <u>acting like Mr. High and Mighty Big Shot</u>. I heard he even put a down payment on a new house. Well, he'd better <u>not count his chickens before they hatch</u> with this company. It's too volatile. But then again, he can always <u>fall back on</u> his mom. She <u>bails him out</u> of any mess he ever gets himself into.

8) I'm going to have to <u>call it a night</u>. I'm totally <u>maxed out</u>. If I do any more work I'm going to turn into a <u>basketcase</u>. I know we're at the final <u>countdown</u> and that we're getting <u>down to the wire</u>, but if I don't <u>hit the sack</u> and <u>snooze</u> for a few hours, believe me, I won't be <u>faking</u> it if you think I'm <u>playing dumb</u> if my work is <u>off by a long shot</u>!

9) Ten sets of volleyball...Wow—how fun! You sure <u>played hard</u> today. How's your shoulder? Is it <u>acting up</u> from all the exercise? Would you like me to <u>play doctor</u> and massage it for you? Oh, I just made some fresh ravioli. Go ahead—<u>knock yourself out</u>. Have as much as you'd like. There is some cold beer in the <u>fridge</u> too.

10) I knew you weren't going to <u>go through with</u> your <u>breakup</u>. You've got to learn to <u>stand up for</u> yourself! He <u>calls your bluff</u> every time and manages to talk you out of whatever you think you should do by <u>promising you the sun, moon, and stars</u>, which you <u>fall for</u> every time. So you should <u>play hard-to-get</u> for a little while to keep him <u>on his best behavior</u>. Yet you know eventually he'll <u>show his true colors</u> and <u>play around</u> again. He'll <u>stand you up</u>, and

you'll <u>call him on it again</u>. It's <u>a vicious circle</u> because you know you can't <u>count on</u> him. You two are <u>playing games</u> with each other. You've got to <u>take a stand</u>!

■ **EXPRESSION LOG:** (1) Choose any 15 expressions from this chapter to practice by writing original sentences, then (2) add two new expressions that you hear. Follow the New Expression Guide in Appendix A.

Look over the list of expressions below before listening to the story. Select the expressions which best paraphrase each part of the story. Some hints are provided. You must use ALL of the expressions one time only. Check them off as you listen.

lightened up	on their case	call their bluff
call off	have a shot at	through the grapevine
got it together	a tough act to follow	knocked on wood
came out smelling like a rose	calling the shots	fall back on
were playing hardball	count on	decent
crooked	a glutton for punishment	a hunch

1. The government and university administrators _____ with the students. They should have _____ and allowed the students to express their opinions.

2. The students had to _____ their demonstration because they didn't want to get kicked out of school. However, they knew people would hear their message _____ because they could _____ the university radio station to support them.

3. However, they were worried that the administration would get _____ if the university radio station aired their views. But they found out that they could _____ another popular radio station if the school gave them a hard time..

4. Both radio station hosts had _____ that many people would be interested in hearing what the students had to say. So many people called the radio stations requesting more information! The students were _____.

5. After listening to the students on the radio, Mr. Daner decided the _____ thing to do would be to open negotiations between the students and the government. He wanted the students to _____ fighting for something they believed in. Because of Mr. Daner's effort, the university almost _____.

6. But a few university administrators were _____. They tried to stop Mr. Daner from supporting the students by threatening him. However, public opinion favored the students. Mr. Daner _____ that would continue because he didn't want to be _____ and have his career destroyed.

7. For the debate, all the government, small business owners and students prepared a lot and really _____. The government wanted to look like they were in control by _____, but the students were able to _____ every time they said something that didn't make sense.

Rules—Go to start. Roll the die. If you get:
Mark your place by writing your name in the boxes.

1-statement question	2- tag question	3-retell what the last person said or go to 6
4-information question	5-negative question	6-your choice!

Start here	1. through the	2. play hardball	3. decent	4. lighten up	5. fall back on
6. play hard-to-get	7. fall for	8. learn something the hard way	9. knock on wood	10. a tough act to follow	11. act up
12. crooked	13. a glutton for punishment	14. Give something a shot	15. a hunch	16. count someone in/out	17. on/off someone's case
18. count on	19. call the shots	20. come out smelling like a rose	21. call off	22. a basketcase	23. a shot in the dark
24. play around	25. call someone's bluff	26. clean up one's act	27. play the game	28. don't count your chickens before they hatch	29. play dumb (but start again!)

CHAPTER

7

wiped out

burn your bridges

touchy

practical joke

pull something off

a taste of your own medicine

the runaround

bail someone out

pumped up

draw the line

cranky

catch off guard

a one-track mind

carry weight

gripe

PART I

Work It Out!

Student Group 1

Learn the meanings of the following five expressions by completing the exercises. Work with Student Group 1 or by yourself.

■ **GUESS** the meanings of the five expressions.

1) You don't want to **burn your bridges**, so you'll have to be tactful.

2) Don't ask Nicki about her accent. She's a little **touchy** about it because she's tired of people always asking where she is from.

3) Everyone in the office conspired to play a **practical joke** on Kim while she was out of town. She was completely taken by surprise when she got back!

4) We were able to see the sights, go shopping, finish our business, and make it to the airport on time. We **pulled it off**!

5) Give him **a taste of his own medicine**! Do exactly what he would do!

■ **CHECK OUT** the definitions and examples of the expressions.

1) **burn one's bridges**—destroy a relationship (business or personal), lose an opportunity.
I don't care if I burn my bridges. I don't want to be associated with them in any way, shape, or form!

2) **touchy**—overly sensitive.
Whatever you do, don't bring up politics. It's a very touchy topic around here.

3) **practical joke**—a planned trick or prank to fool someone.
On April Fool's Day many people play practical jokes on each other just for laughs.

4) **pull something off**—successfully do something difficult.
If we pull this off, they'll be begging for our business!

5) **a taste of one's own medicine**—treat someone the same as they treat others, usually done for revenge or to teach someone a lesson.
I don't want to do this, but I have to give you a taste of your own medicine. You need to know how I feel when you always change your mind at the last minute.

■ **QUICK FIX**—Match the expressions to the words that are similar.

1) high-strung   _____practical joke

2) get even   _____burn one's bridges

3) wisecrack   _____pull something off

4) ruin   _____touchy

5) achieve   _____a taste of one's own medicine

■ **CLOZE IT**—Use one of the above expressions to complete the sentences. Be sure to pay attention to any necessary grammatical changes.

1) I'm not going to rush and worry about being late because she is never on time anyway. I'll give _____ and make her wait for me!

2) I don't know how many of you schemed to play this _____ on me, but you sure had me fooled! I'll get even!

3) I know you're angry with them, but you should try not _____ because you never know what may happen in the future.

4) I'm a bit _____ today because I have too much work to do, but don't take it the wrong way—OK?!

5) He _____ his fifth gas station robbery before he got caught.

■ **SENSE OR NONSENSE**—With your classmates, discuss these sentences and decide if they do or don't make sense.

1) I burned my bridges, so I can always work there again._____

2) It can be very satisfying to give someone a taste of their own medicine, but it can also backfire and have no effect whatsoever._____

3) I pulled it off. I paid my own way through college._____

4) Dieting is a touchy topic for Sara because she has been on so many._____

5) It's fun to plan a practical joke and carry it out._____

■ PLUG IT IN—Use the expressions to replace the underlined words. Make sure to check your grammar. Check the Index/Glossary for words you may not know.

1) That was quite <u>a stunt</u> they pulled on the boss! Finally someone had to tell him the truth because it went a little too far.

2) Congratulations! You <u>came through with flying colors</u>!

3) Robert has been <u>on edge</u> ever since they told him he had to be more careful about what he says.

4) See how you like it! Just <u>a cookie of your own dough</u>.

5) What a bitter divorce. They <u>will never be able to speak to each other again</u>.

Student Group 2

Learn the meanings of the following five expressions by completing the exercises. Work with Student Group 2 or by yourself.

■ **GUESS** the meanings of the five expressions.

1) Be careful if you go shopping there. They usually give tourists the **runaround** about prices.

2) Eric will never grow up because his parents always **bail him out** of every mess he gets himself into.

3) The fans were totally **pumped up** for the championship game!

4) We need to **draw the line** on what is and isn't acceptable to create a comfortable working environment.

5) Don't talk to her right now. She's a little **cranky** because she has an earache again.

■ **CHECK OUT** the definitions and examples of the expressions.

1) **give someone the runaround**—be indirect with someone to avoid or delay something.
   I tried to find out when my computer would be ready, but the repair shop gave me the runaround.

2) **bail someone out of something**—help someone out of a difficult situation that they cause themselves.
   I swear I'll never do that again—I promise! Thanks for bailing me out.

3) **pumped up**—feel excited.
   The teacher had all the students pumped up and ready to practice idioms!

4) **draw the line**—set limits or boundaries.
   I had to draw the line and refuse her when she asked me to bail her out again.

5) **cranky**—irritable, short-tempered.
   Don't talk to him when he's hungry. He gets a bit cranky.

■ **QUICK FIX**—Match the expressions to the words that are similar.

1) aid   _____draw the line

2) restrict   _____give the runaround

3) grumpy   _____pumped up

4) enthusiastic   _____bail someone out

5) put off   _____cranky

■ **CLOZE IT**—Use one of the above expressions to complete the sentences. Be sure to pay attention to any necessary grammatical changes.

1) We couldn't invite everyone we wanted to because our house is too small, so we had to _____.

2) Chris is very _____ in the morning. He needs at least an hour to wake up.

3) Linda comes and goes as she pleases and does whatever she wants because she knows her family _____ if she has any problems.

4) The salesman had the couple completely _____ about buying that beautiful, brand new car!

5) It didn't take me long to figure out they were _____ whenever I asked for the bottom-line price.

■ **SENSE OR NONSENSE**—With your classmates, discuss these sentences and decide if they do or don't make sense.

1) How pleasant it can be to work with cranky colleagues._____

2) If you get the runaround, you can usually finish things faster._____

3) Avid skiers get pumped up whenever it snows!_____

4) Responsible people always ask to get bailed out._____

5) Sometimes it's tough to draw the line with people you love._____

■ **PLUG IT IN**—Use the expressions to replace the underlined words. Make sure to check your grammar. Check the Index/Glossary for words you may not know.

1) That consulting company always <u>beats around the bush with their clients</u>. It's a wonder they've stayed in business as long as they have!

2) My neighbor is so <u>grouchy</u>. He has never said hello in the five years I've lived here. Maybe I'll shock him and give him some chocolate.

3) We all felt really <u>motivated to learn</u> about the new software after the demonstration.

4) Many new couples miscommunicate because they haven't learned how to <u>set limits</u> with each other.

5) I'll <u>help you out</u> this time, but don't count on me next time.

Student Group 3

Learn the meanings of the following five expressions by completing the exercises. Work with Student Group 3 or by yourself.

■ **GUESS** the meanings of the five expressions.

1) Oh! You **caught me off guard**. I didn't know you were here!

2) We were completely **wiped out** after getting back from our trip to Europe.

3) He should change his name to Mr. Money. That's right—he has **a one-track mind**.

4) Rosa's not the boss, but she **carries a lot of weight**.

5) Bradley always seems to have something to **gripe** about, so I'd take what he says with a grain of salt.

■ **CHECK OUT** the definitions and examples of the expressions.

1) **catch someone off guard**—surprise or alert someone.
I was caught off guard by the directness of his questions.

2) **wipe out**—remove, destroy, make exhausted.
Corporations have been wiping out small businesses.

3) **a one-track mind**—be motivated for or fixated on one thing.
I can tell you what he'll want to do on the weekend because he has a one-track mind. He'll only want to hit the bars.

4) **carry weight**—be influential.
Even though Queen Elizabeth II is only supposed to be a figurehead, she really carries a lot of weight when it comes to any major decision making.

5) **gripe**—complain.
You have every reason to gripe. I'd be upset too!

■ **QUICK FIX**—Match the expressions to the words that are similar.

1) important _____catch someone off guard

2) max out _____gripe

3) startle _____carry weight

4) moan _____have a one-track mind

5) obsess _____wipe out

■ **CLOZE IT**—Use one of the above expressions to complete the sentences. Be sure to pay attention to any necessary grammatical changes.

1) Don't worry about what he says. He doesn't _____ around here even though he acts like he does.

2) To finish your degree, you should develop _____ about studying and forget your social life for awhile.

3) The plumber _____ this morning. I thought he was coming over to fix the sink later!

4) The huge wave _____ the surfer, but fortunately he wasn't hurt.

5) Bill always _____ about the computers not being fast enough.

■ **SENSE OR NONSENSE**—With your classmates, discuss these sentences and decide if they do or don't make sense.

1) Someone people love to get together and gripe._____

2) If a cop catches you off guard while you're speeding, you'll probably get a ticket._____

3) Deforestation is wiping out many invaluable plants that have important medicinal properties._____

4) The vice-president doesn't usually carry much weight in the government._____

5) Computer nerds usually have one-track minds._____

■ **PLUG IT IN**—Use the expressions to replace the underlined words. Make sure to check your grammar. Check the Index/Glossary for words you may not know.

1) I had no idea what to say when I ran into my boss at a bar during happy hour.

2) Nadine can always find something to whine about. She is never satisfied.

3) Sean's opinion is pretty powerful around the office.

4) Ayaz isn't a very well-rounded person. All he likes to do is go to the gym and pump iron.

5) The Padres defeated the Giants with a grand-slam victory in the game last night.

Questions to Ask Someone from Student Group 1

Ask Student 1 the following questions. He or she will tell you the answers. You should write down the answers. Student 1 can look at pages 112-114 to find the answers.

■ **TELL ME:** Ask Student 1 the following questions to get the expressions.

1) What is another word for uptight?_____

2) Is there an expression similar to get away with?_____

3) How can I say I'm going to get even?_____

4) What is an expression that means to destroy a relationship?_____

5) What do you call a planned joke not meant to cause harm?_____

■ **MAKE THIS MAKE SENSE:** Ask Student 1 to change these sentences to make sense.

1) It's easy to make jokes with a touchy person.

2) He gave me a taste of my own medicine by doing the opposite of what I would have done.

3) Practical jokes rarely crack up the people who plan them.

4) The swimmer didn't pull off setting a new world record, so he won a gold medal.

5) I care a lot about this job, so I'm going to burn my bridges with the people I work with after I quit.

Questions to Ask Someone from Student Group 2

Ask Student 2 the following questions. He or she will tell you the answers. You should write down the answers. Student 2 can look at pages 115-117 to find the answers.

■ **TELL ME:** Ask Student 2 the following questions to get the expressions.

1) Is there an expression that means someone always gets out of trouble because someone else helps them?_____

2) How can I say I'm really jazzed about something?_____

3) What is a way to say you think someone isn't being direct with you?_____

4) What is another word for grumpy or irritable?_____

5) How do you express that you want to set limits?_____

■ **MAKE THIS MAKE SENSE:** Ask Student 2 to change these sentences to make sense.

1) If you're on a tight budget, you don't have to draw the line on your spending.

2) I usually feel tired whenever I get pumped up about doing something.

3) It must be nice to have a kid who expects to get bailed out of trouble.

4) If someone gives me the runaround, I know I can trust what they say.

5) Being cranky is one of my favorite moods.

Questions to Ask Someone from Student Group 3

Ask Student 3 the following questions. He or she will tell you the answers. You should write down the answers. Student 3 can look at pages 118-119 to find the answers.

■ **TELL ME:** Ask Student 3 following questions to get the expressions.

1) How can you say that someone unexpectedly surprises you when you're not ready?_____

2) What is another way to say complain?_____

3) Is there a way to describe someone who has some influence?_____

4) What is another way to say you feel exhausted?_____

5) How can you describe someone who only thinks about one thing?_____

■ **MAKE THIS MAKE SENSE:** Ask Student 3 to change these sentences to make sense.

1) Tigers and pandas will never be wiped out off the face of the earth.

2) If you have a one-track mind, you're probably a great conversationalist.

3) To learn the ropes, you don't have to know who carries the weight.

4) Listening to people constantly gripe about this, that, and the other is very relaxing.

5) It's great to be caught off guard during an important job interview.

Students 1—2—3

Before you begin the Halftime Activities, you must first complete pages 112-122. These activities are designed to get you to think about and discuss any extended meaning and use of the expressions you have just studied.

■ **EXPRESSION GUIDE:** With your classmates or with a native speaker, look at the Expression Guide below to find out if there is any information to add about the expressions. Write down anything interesting you discover. You can use some of the questions below to get started:

1. Do you use these expressions? Why or why not?

2. Are there any other meanings related to the expressions?

3. Is there any special way to say these expressions?

4. Do you know how these expressions may have originated?

EXPRESSION GUIDE

burn one's bridges	touchy	practical joke	pull something off	give someone a taste of their own medicine
the runaround _slang_	bail someone out _slang_	pumped up _slang_	draw the line	cranky
catch someone off guard	wiped out _slang_	a one-track mind	carry weight	gripe

■ **FIND OUT MORE:** Below is more information about the meanings of some of the expressions as well as a few grammar tips.

1) touchy—There are a few other interesting expressions containing the word **touch**. If you **touch up** a photo, it means you remove the imperfections. If you **touch on** something, you briefly mention it. If someone's service **can't be touched**, it means it is superior to similar service. If someone is **touchy-feely**, they are too concerned about other people's feelings. Finally, if someone says

they **wouldn't touch something with a ten-foot pole**, it means they would stay away from it. Use an appropriate form of touch in the sentences below:

a) This deal can't be beat! There's no comparison. It _____.

b) The speaker barely _____ the most controversial issues.

c) I'd like to have this antique painting _____.

d) That is a real can of worms. I _____.

e) That teacher is too sugary for me. She's very _____.

2) **pull something off**—There are many expressions with **pull**. Here are just a few more.

Read the examples below and write a definition for the underlined expressions.

a) I know you're feeling really uptight right now, but you've got to <u>pull yourself together</u> before the meeting.

_____

b) OK—the joke is over. We were just <u>pulling your leg</u>. We sure had you fooled, didn't we?! You really fell for it!

_____

c) I'm sure they're up to no good because I don't know how they found out about the stock price before we did. I bet they <u>pulled a fast one</u> knowing how crooked they are.

_____

3) **the runaround**—As a phrasal verb, the expression **run around** has three meanings. Read the examples below and match the underlined expressions to the definitions.

a) Louise likes to <u>run around with</u> her theater group. They're a good crowd.   ___cheat on

b) I was <u>running around</u> town this morning doing errands.   ___hang out

c) We think he's <u>running around on</u> her.   ___move around anxiously

d) What a crazy day! I've been <u>running around like a headless chicken</u>.   ___go from place to place

4) **draw the line**—What **line of work** are you in? What would you do if your job were **on the line**? How would you react if someone told you that you were **out of line**? How many hours a week are you **online**? Have you ever had to speak bluntly and **lay it on the line**? Has someone ever flattered you by **feeding you a line?** Do **one-liners** make you laugh? Check out the examples below and decide which expressions best fit.

a) Look. I have to _____ with you and tell it like it really is.

(be straight, direct)

b) How do you like your _____?

(profession, occupation)

c) I'm getting a busy signal. She must be _____.

(connected to a server)

d) His behavior was clearly _____. We were all shocked.

(inappropriate)

e) Robin Williams is famous for his _____.

(short witty jokes)

f) He _____, and I fell for it. He told me I was the

(deliberate flattery)

most beautiful woman he had ever seen.

g) Juliet loved Romeo so much that she _____ her life _____ for him.

(put at risk)

5) catch someone off guard—What do you think it means to be **on guard**? How about to **let your guard down** or **keep your guard up**? You can probably guess! Also, in Chapter 1, you learned a few expressions with **catch**. Here are three more expressions: **catch one's eye**, **catch one's breath**, and **catch someone red-handed**. Read the examples below and match the expressions to the definitions.

a) You'd better be <u>on guard</u> if you drive through that neighborhood at night.   ___take a break, relax

b) Once he <u>let his guard down</u>, he fell in love.   ___be aware

c) <u>Keep your guard up</u> during the negotiations. Be sure you understand everything clearly.   ___attract

d) I'm so glad it's Friday so I can <u>catch my breath</u> after such a busy week.   ___found guilty

e) The chocolate truffle cake <u>caught my eye</u>.   ___be alert

f) He couldn't deny that he stole it. He was busted! He got <u>caught red-handed</u>.   ___become vulnerable

6) a one-track mind—If someone has their **mind in the gutter**, they are thinking vulgar thoughts. If you give someone **a piece of your mind**, you tell them what you think very frankly and directly. If something **blows your mind**, this means you feel astonished about something. Look at the sentences below and fill in the blanks with the best expressions.

a) That's the last time I'm going to let Bruno get away with his sarcastic remarks. I'm going to _____.

b) Marveling at the ancient, giant redwood trees _____.

c) Bob wants to go to another sleazy bar. He really has _____.

7) carry weight—While **carry weight** means to have influence, **carry your own weight** means that you can take care of yourself—that you do your fair share of work. You can also **carry the ball**, which means you are the person who takes on the most difficult or challenging assignment. The phrasal verb **carry on** has a few important meanings: it can mean to continue after an interruption, to behave in a foolish or silly way, or to exaggerate. One last expression worth mentioning is **carry a torch** for someone, which means that you continue to love someone who doesn't have the same feeling for you. Match the expression underlined sentences to the corresponding words on the right.

a)   She <u>carried her own weight</u> throughout college.   ___capable of completing tough tasks

b)   My colleagues <u>were carrying on</u> by singing opera and dancing on their desks because it was the last day of the term!   ___persevere

c)   Roxanne is the one who <u>carries the ball</u> at work. If she left, we would need three people to replace her.   ___independent

d)   Even though we've been divorced for two years, my ex-husband still <u>carries a torch</u> for me.   ___melodramatic

e)   All she did was scratch her arm, and she is <u>carrying on</u> like she needs stitches.   ___goof off

f)   Although the earthquake destroyed the city, people had no choice but to <u>carry on</u>.   ___unrequited love

■ **READ** the following and discuss the probable meanings of the underlined expressions. Circle any key words or phrases that help you to understand the meaning(s).

1)   Louis is <u>cranky</u> today because Sue finally <u>gave him a taste of his own medicine</u>. He expected her to stay late again to finish his part of the work, but she did her <u>fair share</u> and then <u>took off</u> right before he usually does. This morning he started <u>whining</u> about the work not being done, and asked her, in a sarcastic tone of voice, if she cared about their teamwork. She <u>stood up to him</u> and told him that she wasn't going to <u>bail him out</u> anymore. She said she <u>had caught</u> him <u>goofing off</u> playing video games and surfing the net when he should have been working. She also said she was <u>fed up with</u> his two-hour lunch breaks and his constant <u>bragging</u> about how his workout at the gym went. He was speechless! I suppose he <u>figured</u> that he could keep <u>schmoozing</u> her into doing his work for him, but she finally <u>drew the line</u> and <u>gave him a piece of her mind</u>.

2)   I think Erik, the new guy, is <u>carrying a little torch</u> for Sofia. I <u>caught him completely off guard</u> yesterday <u>checking her out</u>. He noticed that I noticed, and he <u>turned bright red</u>. I winked and told him that <u>my lips were sealed</u>. Anyway, this morning he asked me to <u>find out</u> if <u>she's seeing anyone</u>. I think he's <u>a man on a mission</u>. He's got <u>a one-track mind</u> to <u>find out</u> as much as possible about Sofia before he <u>musters up</u> the courage to <u>ask her out</u>. So, I think he's asking me because I know the crowd she <u>runs around with</u>. He wants to know what she's interested in because he <u>figures</u> she probably gets <u>hit on</u> all the time. He doesn't want <u>to come off</u> sounding like just another <u>jerk feeding her a line</u>.

3)   I'm completely <u>wiped out</u>! I've been <u>running around like a headless chicken</u> all week <u>dealing with</u> the <u>red tape</u> to file this insurance claim. I had no idea it would take this long. What's worse is that I have to constantly be <u>on guard</u> because if I miss something, no one will tell me! I feel like they're <u>giving me</u>

the runaround. I have to actually read and understand the fine print. Normally I wouldn't touch this with a ten-foot pole, but I realize I'm on my own. I've got to carry my own weight because what you don't know can hurt you as far as understanding the policy is concerned. I'm going to toughen up and stick it out. I don't care how many times I have to ask the same questions. I want to feel certain that they won't pull a fast one and not pay me the amount of my policy.

4) Laura caught Alex red-handed online checking out yet another porno site! This time she said it's really gotten out of hand. What happened was that she had forgotten a disk she needed for work, so she went home during her lunch break to get it. Alex was in the bathroom when she got home, so he wasn't sitting at the computer. She said it blew her mind to see what he was looking at! It's all hardcore. He's really got his mind in the gutter. After that, they got into a huge fight. He accused her of spying on him, and now he's giving her the silent treatment. That's really messed up! He's been depressed because he hasn't had much luck finding work, but that's no excuse to carry on like a sleazy jerk with his wife. In fact, almost every time she even touches on the topic of his work, he blows up. She's going to have to lay it on the line with him and tell him to quit taking out his frustrations on her; otherwise their marriage may fall apart.

5) Carlos is pumped up about the new translation contract he landed with the government. He's going to translate Web sites from English to Spanish. He's had his heart set on this type of work for ages. He has a fantastic reputation as a translator/interpreter because he can quickly spot any slight error and touch it up. In fact, the quality of his work can't be touched. It even caught the eye of the Deputy Secretary of Agriculture in Washington, D.C. He's been doing a top-notch job working like crazy for years. He finally got the break he deserves. This is just the beginning of a great new turn in his career!

6) Larry's been running around hanging out almost every night with the good old boys doing the guy thing. Once his girlfriend, Betty, let her guard down and gave him an inch, but he took a mile. She told him to go ahead and have some fun with his buddies, but she didn't mean for him to go out so often. But the real problem is whenever she wants to go out with her friends, he gives her a hard time. He's a possessive guy. It's become such a touchy topic between them that Betty has decided to take the bull by the horns and even the score with him a little. She and a few of her friends have made plans to go to Hawaii. That ought to give him a little taste of his own medicine, but then again it could backfire. She should be able to do what she wants to do, just like he does. Dealing with possessive people is really tough, especially when you love them.

7) I told Bobby to be careful not to burn his bridges with the school administrators and put his certificate on the line because he's been so flaky about attendance and tardiness. He's been able to get away with being late for a little while because he is a friendly, bright student who catches on very quickly. But intelligence can take you only so far. If you're late, you're late. If you're absent, you're absent—end of story. You can only schmooze your teachers with your excuses so much. It depends on how touchy-feely they are or aren't. They might let some of the tardies slide, but they have to check the absences and stick to the attendance policy.

8) It's tax time again. Time to pay <u>Uncle Sam</u>! Personally I think the tax system is way <u>out of line</u>. There's a lot to <u>gripe</u> about. Every year the more I work, the more I pay, and I never seem to <u>get ahead</u>. I used to do my taxes at the beginning of the year, but now I <u>put them off</u> until the last minute because I think the system punishes people who work hard. Whether you're married or single, you don't get any <u>tax breaks</u> unless you become self-employed, purchase property, have some <u>dependents</u>, or put your money into <u>tax-deferred</u> plans. Or you can just work <u>under the table</u>! That way you won't pay any taxes at all! Just don't <u>get caught</u>! I know there are plenty of other ways to pay fewer taxes, but you've got to be <u>savvy</u> about it. Or, you have to pay an accountant who knows the loopholes to do them for you. Anyway, it's almost <u>April 15</u>, the tax deadline It's time to <u>carry on</u>, <u>pull myself together</u>, quit my <u>whining</u>, and <u>face</u> the inevitable. As Benjamin Franklin once said, "There are only two things certain in life: death and taxes."

9) Amanda has got to slow down and <u>catch her breath</u>. She <u>carries a lot of weight</u> at work. So many people <u>count on</u> her. But what a lot of people don't know is that she is also <u>carrying the ball</u> at home. She has a huge family and right now they are <u>going through</u> a lot. Her husband recently had knee surgery. Her 84-year old mother-in-law has severe arthritis, and her great-aunt has Alzheimers. And that's only the half of it. She has four kids too! She's truly extraordinary because she is capable of <u>handling</u> many things at once, but sooner or later all this <u>running around</u>, doing <u>errands</u>, and taking care of everyone is going to <u>catch up with her</u>. I don't know how she <u>pulls it off</u> every day with her mountain of responsibilities. I hope things <u>settle down</u> for her soon because no one can <u>keep up this pace</u>.

10) Michael is <u>hysterical</u>. He can <u>crack anyone up</u>. He's always full of great <u>one-liners</u>. They just fly out of his mouth naturally. He can take almost any situation and make it funny. Once I asked him how he does it, and he told me that he <u>grew up</u> in a family that thrived on <u>pulling each other's legs</u>. He said they would sit around the dinner table and have contests to see who could <u>come up with</u> the best jokes. So, if you want to play any <u>practical jokes</u> on anyone, just ask Michael. He's the expert! He'll give you lots of great ideas.

■ **EXPRESSION LOG:** (1) Choose any 15 expressions from this chapter to practice by writing original sentences, then (2) add two new expressions that you hear. Follow the New Expression Guide in Appendix A.

BINGO: Choose 24 of the following expressions and write them anywhere in the Bingo squares. Check off your selections. You will then listen to some descriptions of the expressions. If your expression is described, put an X through the box. As soon as you cross off five expressions in a row, horizontally, vertically, or diagonally, shout out Bingo! You will then have to verify that your choices were correct, so take short notes to justify your selections.

__burn your bridges	__touchy	__practical joke	__a taste of their own medicine
__pull it off	__put it off	__one-track mind	__lay it on the line
__run around with	__pumped up	__drew the line	__caught him off guard
__bailed me out	__cranky	__can't be touched	__pulled a fast one
__carry the weight	__gripe	__out of line	__touch it with a 10-foot pole
__feed them a line	__wiped out	__blow my mind	__stand up to them
__fed up with	__goofing off	__fine print	__falling for something
__your lips are sealed	__stick it out	__got out of hand	__a piece of your mind

		BINGO		

PART V

The Chat Room

Trivia Challenge: In a small group, take turns answering the questions in the boxes to see what you remember from Chapter 7. Choose one category and try to finish it before moving on to the next. If no one knows the answer, take a guess, or ask another classmate or your teacher. You can even ask a native speaker.

	Synonyms	Same Expression, Different Meaning	High Profile Expression	What's The Difference...?	For Adults Only?
1.	What are two other words for **gripe**?	Give three meanings of **run around**.	Name and explain three expressions with the word **touch**.	between **online** and **on the line**?	Explain what it means to **swear**.
2.	Name three other words for **cranky**.	Give two meanings of **carry on**.	Name and explain three expressions with the word **pull**.	**carry weight** and **carry your weight**?	What can **hard-core** be used to describe?
3.	What are some similar words for **practical joke**?	Give two meanings of **put off**.	Name and explain three expressions with the word **catch**.	**touch on** and **touch up**?	Why do some adults become **touchy-feely**?
4.	What are two other ways to say **touchy**?	Give two meanings of catch someone **off guard**.	Name and explain three expressions with the word **mind**.	**keep your guard up** and **be on guard**?	Why are **tax breaks** important for adults?
5.	What is another way to say **lay it on the line**?	Give two meanings of **wipe out**.	Name and explain three expressions with the word **line**.	**mess up** and **be messed up**?	What happens if adults get **out of line**?

CHAPTER

8

an ivory tower

slick

the back burner

chew out

a comeback

get up the nerve

below the belt

move on

lame

make ends meet

bounce something off someone

wacky

a geek

add up

ahead of the game

Student Group 1

Learn the meanings of the following five expressions by completing the exercises. Work with Student Group 1 or by yourself.

■ **GUESS** the meanings of the five expressions.

1) Your new car is really **slick**! I bet you paid a pretty penny for it.

2) I'm going to put this project **on the back burner** for awhile since it doesn't have to be finished until next month.

3) I had to **chew out** my puppy for chewing up my gorgeous new shoes!

4) Tina Turner made one of the greatest **comebacks** in show business history.

5) Diane **got up the nerve** to quit her job to go full force into her own business.

■ **CHECK OUT** the definitions and examples of the expressions.

1) **slick**—great, smooth, stylish; clever in a sly or tricky way.
   When Mr. Clinton was president, his nickname was "Slick Willy" because, amidst all the controversies, he seems to come out of smelling like a rose.

2) **the back burner**—put off doing, delay, not a priority.
   Don't leave homework on the back burner for too long. You might run out of time.

3) **chew out**—scold, get angry at.
   My supervisor didn't like the way I spoke to him, so he chewed me out.

4) **a comeback**—success after a dormant period; witty remark.
   Stand-up comedians have to be good at making comebacks in front of a live audience.

5) **get up the nerve**—stick your neck out, be brave.
   Nho got up the nerve and told his parents he was going to study what he wanted, not what they wanted him to study regardless of whether or not they cut him off financially.

■ **QUICK FIX**—Match the expressions to the words that are similar.

1) procrastinate   ___get up the nerve

2) repartee   ___chew out

3) gutsy   ___the back burner

4) shrewd   ___comeback

5) bawl out   ___slick

■ **CLOZE IT**—Use one of the above expressions to complete the sentences. Be sure to pay attention to any necessary grammatical changes.

1) Sophie _____ and went skydiving.

2) Bill looks rather _____ in his new suit.

3) Steve's business flopped, but he _____ and is doing really well now.

4) You're so self-centered. You do whatever you want, but whenever it comes to what I want, you put me _____.

5) I had to _____ my kid for not being careful when he crossed the street.

■ **SENSE OR NONSENSE**—With your classmates, discuss these sentences and decide if they do or don't make sense.

1) Joe is a really slick salesman. He could sell refrigerators in the Arctic._____

2) Diane got up her nerve to confront the situation, so she went home and crawled under the covers._____

3) It's fun to get chewed out in front of other people._____

4) He's a great boyfriend. He never puts her on the back burner._____

5) Dennis may be on the quiet side, but he always has a comeback._____

■ **PLUG IT IN**—Use the expressions to replace the underlined words. Make sure to check your grammar. Check the Index/Glossary for words you may not know.

1) My third-grade teacher once <u>admonished me</u> because she thought I'd said a bad word.

2) The flamenco dancers were so <u>sleek</u> that they made the dancing look easy.

3) This might take a long time to process, so you'd better not <u>leave it till the last minute</u>.

4) Joseph <u>has a lot of chutzpa</u> to ask the president such a direct question.

5) Oscar is ready to <u>rumble again</u> after his unlucky dry spell.

Student Group 2

Learn the meanings of the following five expressions by completing the exercises. Work with Student Group 2 or by yourself.

■ **GUESS** the meanings of the five expressions.

1) So much of the negative campaigning really **hit below the belt**.

2) It's time to **move on**. We have to kiss this proposal goodbye.

3) The movie was so **lame** that we almost walked out!

4) Many politicians live in an **ivory tower**. They really can't relate to the plight of the working class.

5) When inflation is on the rise, it's hard to **make ends meet**.

■ **CHECK OUT** the definitions and examples of the expressions.

1) **hit below the belt**—unfair or inappropriate remark, out of line.
   Sometimes a joke can go too far and hit below the belt.

2) **move on**—carry on after an important change or decision, don't look back.
   It was a sad break-up, but they both had to move on and start a new life.

3) **lame**—inconsiderate; inadequate; stupid.
   They asked me to work for them again, but they didn't want to pay me as much as before. On top of that, there is more work this time. That's pretty lame!

4) **an ivory tower**—a sheltered life unlike most other people's reality.
   Many people in academic circles live in an ivory tower.

5) **make ends meet**—ability to afford life with the money you earn.
   She has to work two jobs to make ends meet.

■ **QUICK FIX**—Match the expressions to the words that are similar.

1) thoughtless   ___move on

2) cheap shot   ___an ivory tower

3) reconstruct   ___lame

4) have enough   ___hit below the belt

5) protected   ___make ends meet

■ **CLOZE IT**—Use one of the above expressions to complete the sentences. Be sure to pay attention to any necessary grammatical changes.

1) My car was supposed to have been ready two days ago. This is_____.

2) Her parents wanted to give her the best of everything, but she wasn't cut out for _____.

3) If we buy this house, it'll be tough _____.

4) I really had a great time studying here, but it's time _____.

5) Your remark _____. That was just plain mean.

■ **SENSE OR NONSENSE**—With your classmates, discuss these sentences and decide if they do or don't make sense.

1) When you're on your own for the first time, it's tough to make ends meet._____

2) He kept falling back into the same routine because he had moved on._____

3) You have it made if you live in an ivory tower._____

4) He's so tacky. He always hits below the belt when he tries to get even._____

5) We have a three-day weekend coming up. How lame!_____

■ **PLUG IT IN**—Use the expressions to replace the underlined words. Make sure to check your grammar. Check the Index/Glossary for words you may not know.

1) Natalie <u>leads a very pampered life</u>. She doesn't do anything that doesn't suit her fancy.

2) Whenever Pascal lost a tennis match, he wouldn't talk to anyone. He's <u>a sore loser</u>.

3) Tom's deceit was tough to swallow, but we had to <u>leave it behind</u>.

4) The minimum wage isn't enough for people to <u>live within their means</u>.

5) I wonder why Eileen always <u>has to bring up my past</u> in front of people we've just met.

Student Group 3

Learn the meanings of the following five expressions by completing the exercises. Work with Student Group 3 or by yourself.

■ **GUESS** the meanings of the five expressions.

1) Let me **bounce this idea off you**. Tell me what you think, OK?

2) She wears **the wackiest** clothes! She even has a dress made of credit cards!

3) From nerd to **geek**! What is happening to our little egghead?

4) His story doesn't make sense. It just **doesn't add up**.

5) If you study hard now, you'll be **ahead of the game** later.

■ **CHECK OUT** the definitions and examples of the expressions.

1) **bounce ideas off someone**—ask for a suggestion or opinion.
David's in charge of putting together the new computer lab. That's why he's been bouncing so many ideas off us.

2) **wacky**—crazy, zany, off the wall.
This electric brain buzzer sure is a wacky invention. I can't believe it was actually patented!

3) **geek**—a nerdy person who is typically good with computers; a peculiar person; socially unskilled.
George is a self-confessed computer geek. He said he's gone beyond nerdlike behavior. He lives for computer engineering.

4) **add up**—make sense; indicate, result.
Rain followed by heat added up to an ant invasion.

5) **ahead of the game**—forward thinking; too soon; in an advantageous position.
You've already finished? You're way ahead of the game.

■ **QUICK FIX**—Match the expressions to the words that are similar.

1) freaky   ___geek

2) seek advice   ___wacky

3) be logical   ___bounce ideas off someone

4) early   ___add up

5) dweeb   ___ahead of the game

■ **CLOZE IT**—Use one of the above expressions to complete the sentences. Be sure to pay attention to any necessary grammatical changes.

1) I have a big decision to make. Do you mind if I _____?

2) One thing's for sure. You'll never get bored with a _____ person!

3) Oh, I get it. Now that you've explained that, it all _____.

4) Don't ask Ernie about that software! He'll talk your ears off about it for years to come. I know he doesn't seem like _____, but believe me, he is!

5) I need to stay on top of things because I have a lot of projects coming up, so I'm not going to go out this weekend. I've got to _____ for a while.

■ **SENSE OR NONSENSE**—With your classmates, discuss these sentences and decide if they do or don't make sense.

1) Wacky weather is unpredictable._____

2) Leonardo da Vinci was way ahead of the game._____

3) The motive and the evidence all added up._____

4) It's a drag to work with people you can bounce your ideas off._____

5) A geek is to computers what a jock is to sports._____

■ **PLUG IT IN**—Use the expressions to replace the underlined words. Make sure to check your grammar. Check the Index/Glossary for words you may not know.

1) I'd like to <u>hear your input</u>. You can be completely frank with me, ok?

2) Frequent phone calls and little tokens of affection <u>are symbolic of</u> love.

3) He's too much of <u>a freak</u> to work with. He'd never be a good team leader.

4) Jim Carrey's crazy faces are <u>outrageous</u>.

5) The avant-garde artists of the 1920s were <u>very hip</u>.

Questions to Ask Someone from Student Group 1

Ask Student 1 the following questions. He or she will tell you the answers. You should write down the answers. Student 1 can look at pages 132-134 to find the answers.

■ **TELL ME**: Ask Student 1 the following questions to get the expressions.

1) What can you say if you don't feel like doing something but you'll do it later?

   _____

2) Is there an expression to describe a successful return after a period of stagnation?

   _____

3) What's another word for scold?_____

4) How can you describe something that is stylish?_____

5) What's a way to tell someone to stick their neck out?_____

■ **MAKE THIS MAKE SENSE:** Ask Student 1 to change these sentences to make sense.

1) It's OK if you chew out your boss, especially if you want a raise.

2) A klutz is usually very slick.

3) If you can't get up the nerve, I'll take you glacier skiing.

4) Making a comeback must be very disappointing.

5) I don't mind being put on the back burner when something is important to me.

Questions to Ask Someone from Student Group 2

Ask Student 2 the following questions. He or she will tell you the answers. You should write down the answers. Student 2 can look at pages 135-136 to find the answers.

■ **TELL ME:** Ask Student 2 the following questions to get the expressions.

1) How can you describe something that is both dumb and inappropriate?_____

2) What is a way to say that you can pay your own way in life?_____

3) Is there a way to say that someone lives a charmed life?_____

4) What can you call an unfair comment?_____

5) How can you describe that it's time to make a change?_____

■ **MAKE THIS MAKE SENSE:** Ask Student 2 to change these sentences to make sense.

1) If you were a voyeur, you'd probably love to live in an ivory tower.

2) This ruby necklace is one of the lamest gifts I've ever received.

3) It's fun to get hit below the belt in front of people you want to make a good impression on.

4) She decided to move on so she got back together with her ex-husband.

5) Making ends meet using credit cards is a great way to get ahead.

Questions to Ask Someone from Student Group 3

Ask Student 3 the following questions. He or she will tell you the answers. You should write down the answers. Student 3 can look at pages 137-138 to find the answers.

■ **TELL ME:** Ask Student 3 following questions to get the expressions.

1) Is there an expression to describe someone who is more than a nerd?_____

2) What is a way to say something seems to fit or is logical?_____

3) What's a way to ask someone for their opinion about something?_____

4) How can you describe someone who does things early?_____

5) Is there a synonym for nuts, loopy, or off the wall?_____

■ **MAKE THIS MAKE SENSE:** Ask Student 3 to change these sentences to make sense.

1) An average field of work is usually great for a wacky person.

2) I love it when someone continues to bounce the same idea off me when I've already told them what I think.

3) It's really easy to understand things that don't add up.

4) Geeks make great boyfriends because they spend all their time on computers.

5) He loves to stay ahead of the game by putting everything on the back burner.

Students 1—2—3

Before you begin the Halftime Activities, you must first complete pages 132-141. These activities are designed to get you to think about and discuss any extended meaning and usage of the expressions you have just studied.

■ **EXPRESSION GUIDE:** With your classmates or with a native speaker, look at the Expression Guide below to find out if there is any information to add about the expressions. Write down anything interesting you discover. You can use some of the questions below to get started:

1.   Do you use these expressions? Why or why not?

2.   Are there any other meanings related to the expressions?

3.   Is there any special way to say these expressions?

4.   Do you know how these expressions may have originated?

EXPRESSION GUIDE

slick *slang*	the back burner	chew out *slang*	a comeback	get up the nerve
below the belt	move on	lame *slang*	an ivory tower	make ends meet
bounce ideas off someone	wacky *slang*	a geek *slang*	add up	ahead of the game

■ **FIND OUT MORE:** Below is more information about the meanings of some of the expressions as well as a few grammar tips.

1)   **the back burner**—The word **back** is part of many expressions. Look at the sentences below and write a short definition for the underlined expressions.

  a)   The cab driver knew all the <u>back streets</u> in the city, so we beat the traffic. _____

b) You'd better <u>back off</u>. You're putting too much pressure on everyone._____

c) We have a good <u>back up</u> plan in case this one doesn't work out._____

d) She <u>stabbed me in the back</u> with her lies. I thought she was my friend. I'll <u>get back at her</u> for this._____

e) I have <u>back-to-back</u> appointments, so I can't squeeze you in today. Can I <u>get back to you</u> tomorrow?_____

2) **get up the nerve**—You probably remember what it means to **get on one's nerves** from Chapter 2, but do you know what **to have nerve** means? How about to **hit a nerve** or **to have nerves of steel**? Read the examples and select one of the expressions to complete them.

a) Tony always had thick skin. That's why he trained to be a Navy Seal. Now he _____.

b) Reality TV shows sometimes _____ with the public. They cause controversy.

c) Her constant griping about nothing significant _____. I wish she would find something worth complaining about!

d) Norman _____ to say such rude and insulting things, especially for someone as lame as he is!

3) **below the belt**—There are a couple of interesting expressions with the word **belt**. Did you ever **get the belt** when you got in trouble? Have you ever had to **tighten your belt** and save some money? Do you know anyone who can **belt it out** like an opera singer? How many years of work experience do you have **under your belt**? Answer the following questions using one of the above expressions in your answer.

a) Do you ever sing in the shower?_____

b) How long have you been studying English?_____

c) Are you watching your spending these days?_____

d) What happens if you spank a child in your country?_____

4) **move on**—There are lots of expressions that look similar to **move on**. Look at the list below and choose the definitions which best fit the examples.

a) Come on! Let's <u>get a move on</u>!   ___take over

b) That new salesguy is <u>moving in on</u> my territory.   ___traveling

c) People in marketing are constantly <u>on the move</u>.   ___pick up

d) Louis LeBeau <u>is putting the moves on</u> me!   ___hurry

5) **bounce ideas off someone**—You know what it means to bounce a ball, but how about **bounce a check**? Do you know what **a bouncer** does? Have you ever **bounced back**? Use your grammatical knowledge to complete the blanks and then write a short definition.

a) I didn't have enough money in my bank account, so _____.

_____

b) Ronald Reagan got shot, but he _____ to work the following week._____

c) Don't mess with _____. He'll throw you out of the club.

_____

6) add up—Here are three classic expressions containing the word **add**: **add insult to injury**, **add fuel to the fire**, and **add the finishing touches**. Which sentences best describe these expressions?

a) The bride is almost ready. She just needs to apply some lip gloss, put on her garter, and put on her veil._____

b) Everyone is already very upset and on edge. If you start to complain you'll just make everyone angrier._____

c) First he told her she should lose weight, and then he invited her out for some ice cream._____

7) ahead of the game—Here are four more interesting expressions related to the word **game**. If **the game is up**, it's time to quit because you got caught. If you understand **the name of the game**, you know what is important in order to succeed. If you're at a certain **stage of the game**, you're at a particular point in an activity. If someone or something is **fair game**, they deserve to be made fun of or attacked. Use one of the above expressions in the examples below.

a) In real estate, _____ is to sell!

b) At this _____, we'd better check out the reports before we continue.

c) In the world of politics, a person's public record is _____.

d) All right, _____. I know what you're up to.

■ **READ** the following and discuss the probable meanings of the underlined expressions. Circle any key words or phrases that help you to understand the meaning(s).

1) Dennis Rodman sure knows how to bounce a basketball. He definitely knows the name of the game. That's why he was able to get away with all his wacky stunts: his hair colors, his gender-bender clothing, and his wild tattoos. His team put up with him for a long time. They backed him up because he's such an awesome player who contributed to their wins. However, finally they'd had enough of his nervy pranks, and they cut him loose. But Dennis will always be newsworthy. Wherever he is and whatever he does, he'll always be out there!

2) Carlos Santana made one of the greatest comebacks in music history! He was out of the public eye for quite a while, but in 1999 he came out with "Supernatural", and he won 7 Grammys including Record of the Year. It's fantastic because all the years of experience he has under his belt shine through. He collaborated with other great artists like guitarist Eric Clapton and the Mexican rock group Mana. He wrote the song "Smooth" with singer Rob Thomas, and it's no surprise that it got Song of the Year. The songs on "Supernatural" are in both English and Spanish. The artwork is very hip, and so are Carlos's words of praise and gratitude to the people he worked with. But he added the finishing touches by donating all the proceeds to Milagros, a charity he founded years ago for underprivileged children.

3) After the holidays and taxes, it's time for many people to <u>tighten their belts</u> so that they can <u>make ends meet</u> without <u>maxing out</u> their credit cards. They'd better be sure not to <u>bounce any checks</u> either because some banks charge $20 for returned checks! Imagine that—you don't have enough money and then they charge you even more! You better be sure that your bank provides you with overdraft protection. That way if you write a check that isn't covered because you're waiting for a deposit to <u>go through</u>, your bank will protect you. <u>What you don't know about handling money can hurt you</u>. It's wise not to keep it <u>on the back burner</u>. Take the time to learn as much as possible about managing your money!

4) My father could never <u>get up the nerve</u> to <u>give my sister or me the belt</u> even though sometimes we were really bad. I remember one time we did something to upset our parents, and they <u>chewed us out</u>. They told us we were going to <u>get the belt</u> after dinner. So they made us sit through dinner and eat everything. I think they thought by the miserable look on our faces that that was punishment enough. They never did <u>spank</u> us, and we never did the bad thing we did to upset them in the first place again. We <u>learned our lesson</u>: <u>Don't mess with</u> Mom or Dad!

5) I used to have a good friend named Janice. I met her at work, and I thought she was so funny because from time to time she would <u>belt out</u> whatever work we were doing in her loudest operatic voice. She had a really great voice too, and she <u>cracked everyone up</u>. But Janice was always having trouble <u>making ends meet</u>. She loved to cook. In fact, she was a gourmet cook, and she liked to give parties at her house and cook all the food for everyone. This got to be too expensive for her. She <u>maxed out</u> all her credit cards. I used to worry about her because she'd spend her last dime on food. Her boyfriend finally <u>broke up</u> with her over it. He said she was <u>a glutton for punishment</u>. But Janice managed to <u>bounce back</u>. She met a really nice guy named Gary. He was <u>loaded</u>, and he loved to eat. They got married and bought a big house. But the story doesn't end happily. Her newly found wealth and her obsessive tendencies <u>added up to</u> an obsession with her house, car, and clothes. <u>In a nutshell</u>, Janice became a <u>material girl</u> who lives in <u>an ivory tower</u>. She's a prisoner to her image. I don't see her very often anymore because <u>at this stage of the game</u> she <u>gets on my nerves</u> too much. She's <u>lost it</u>.

6) We'd better <u>get a move on</u> if we're going to make it to the airport on time. Let's take the <u>back streets</u> until we can catch the freeway. There'll be <u>back-to-back</u> traffic right now on the main roads. What a shame we can't rely on public transportation in this city. It's so <u>lame</u>. This really <u>hits a nerve</u> with me. How can the local government say that we live in "America's finest city?" They grant building permits for construction companies to <u>move in on</u> and destroy the open space by building more and more homes and condos without consideration for traffic concerns. It's all about making the <u>big bucks</u>. Taking 45 minutes to drive 3 miles <u>doesn't add up</u> to living in "America's finest city."

7) To get a good job in the computer industry, you've got to be a <u>nerd</u>. But becoming a <u>geek</u> requires spending most of your life on the computer to stay <u>ahead of the game</u>. Then you have to prove yourself by outperforming all the nerds. Geeks are respected among the <u>tekkies</u>. If you're a super geek, your company will do anything to make you happy. They'll <u>set you up</u> in your own little <u>ivory</u>

tower at work so that you can actually live there. Your co-workers will have to put up with all your bizarre idiosyncratic habits. The intense race for technology is creating new breeds of people, and everyone is fair game for attack.

8) Queen Elizabeth I of England had to have nerves of steel. She lived in the sixteenth century during a time of great religious conflict. In the beginning of her reign, there were many people in her court who were ready to back stab her to move in on her power. Whenever anyone got caught for treason, they were usually sent to the Tower of London to be beheaded. Because of all the treachery, Elizabeth could bounce her ideas off of very few people. There were also many men who tried to put the moves on her. She realized that she had to focus on England. She became known as the Virgin Queen, and chose to "marry England." Elizabeth was a great leader but a lonely woman. Years later in her reign, she let her guard down and fell for Sir Walter Raleigh. He was her knight in shining armor. He claimed to love her too, but to add insult to injury, he cheated on her. She got back at him by sending him to the Tower. Sometimes it pays to be queen.

P.S. I'm pulling your leg! This historical anecdote isn't entirely true. I made up some of it so that I could use the expressions! In 1575, Sir Walter Raleigh founded the first English colony in the New World, Jamestown. I bet Elizabeth loved him for that! But by 1590, everyone who lived there got wiped out due to starvation. Those first colonists didn't know that they could eat corn.

9) It's spring break, and all the college students are on the move. Most of them are headed for the beach towns to party hard. The bouncers in beach clubs are going to have their hands full handling the kids who get hammered or who just get out of line. They have to break up a lot of fights and throw a lot of people out of the clubs because many of them don't know when to back off. A lot of students also cross the border to party all night long in Mexico. But the Mexican people have gotten fed up with dealing with all the wasted American kids driving around on their streets. To add fuel to the fire, the police on both sides of the border end up throwing the totally ripped ones in the slammer to sleep it off overnight. It must really hit their parents below the belt when they find out how much it costs to bail their precious little angels out of jail!

10) It's time to move on. The game is up. We have a slick idea, but we'll have to hold off on it until we can convince the bank to give us a loan. It's a catch-22. To get a loan, you have to prove that you don't need a loan. But if you didn't need a loan, why would you be asking for one in the first place? Go figure! Does that add up? There's got to be a better way. We'll put this proposal on the back burner and get back to it as soon as we've figured out a way to make it happen. Let's not give up! Everyone says they know it can work, but we have to find someone who will put their money where their mouth is.

■ **EXPRESSION LOG:** (1) Choose any 15 expressions from this chapter to practice by writing original sentences, then (2) add two new expressions that you hear. Follow the New Expression Guide in Appendix A.

Listen to five situations and write all the expressions which correspond. Choose from the list below. Be sure to use ALL the expressions! You can use some more than once. Check them off as you listen and compare your answers with your classmates.

hit a nerve	ivory tower	bounce ideas off someone	get on one's nerves	ahead of the game
hit below the belt	draw the line	slick	lame	make ends meet
make a comeback	add insult to injury	nerves of steel	the back burner	stand up to
wacky	move on	crack up	a geek	add up

SITUATIONS—Write the expressions below:

1)

2)

3)

4)

5)

Call Your Bluff: Roll the die and move to the corresponding box. Look at the expression, and with the straightest face possible, make up a story that can be either true or false. You can use as many expressions as you please in your story, but write your name in the box to mark your place. After telling your story, a classmate will ask you some questions to decide whether you are telling the truth or fibbing. Have fun!

1. slick Names:	2. a bouncer Names:	3. add the finishing touches Names:	4. fair game Names:	5. below the belt Names:
10. bounce an idea off someone Names:	9. chew out Names:	8. back off Names:	7. move on Names:	6. ahead of the game Names:
11. hit a nerve Names:	12. wacky Names:	13. a comeback Names:	14. add up Names:	15. the name of the game Names:
20. back stab Names:	19. an ivory tower Names:	18. get back at Names:	17. the back burner Names:	16. bounce back Names:
21. make ends meet Names:	22. geek Names:	23. get up the nerve Names:	24. move in on Names:	25. lame Names:
30. back up Names:	29. put the moves on Names:	28. bounce a check Names:	27. under your belt Names:	26. have nerve Names:

Target pp. 1-7, 18-23, 20-27	Expanded pp. 11-15, 31-35	In Context pp. 1-38
a break	baby boomers	a chicken
a flake	be bought	a cop
a tip	bent out of shape	a dent
a wimp	buy into	a quack
ask for it	catch	a two-timer
be cut out for	catch-22	back out of
bend over backwards	clueless	beat the odds
buy something	deal	beer belly
catch on	dinks	be made for
cut corners	even out	be with it
deal with	even steven	big time
food for thought	even the score	bro
funky	flake out	c'est la vie
get away with	flaky	come through
get even	funk	do-it-yourself
grow on someone	funky	drop by
guts	generation X	emotional roller coaster
have what it takes	generation Y	fad
in a nutshell	get caught	fair weather friend
jazzed	get on someone's nerves	feed someone's ego
keep/be up on	give me a break	feel like
make out	gut	for real
push one's luck	gutless	fully loaded
schmooze	gutsy	get off on the wrong foot
spaced out	clue	get out of doing something
speak of the devil	in a funk	get the green light
straight	make out	get up on the wrong side of the bed
the whole nine yards	neck	go for
wine and dine	play catch-up	in hot water
yuppie	rub off on someone	make it
	rub someone the wrong way	man
	sources	mouth off
	spill your guts	news junkie
	straight	on one's plate
	take it	pointers
	take something out on someone	pull something off
	those are the breaks	reinvent the wheel
	tip off	scheme
	tip	shallow
	up for	stay/keep in touch
	up to	stoked
	up	the easy way out
	up front	the mob
	watch the submarine races	tough
		turn in
		what's up

PASSWORD: Player 1

- Choose a partner: Player 1 and Player 2
- Player 2: Turn to page 152 without looking at this page.
- Player 1: Look at the list below. Read one of your expressions to Player 2, who will tell you another expression that has a similar meaning. Write it down.
- Take turns with Player 2 until your list is complete.

<table>
<tr><th colspan="2">PLAYER 1</th><th colspan="2">PLAYER 2</th></tr>
<tr><th>Expression</th><th>Synonym</th><th>Expression</th><th>Synonym</th></tr>
<tr><td>a tip</td><td></td><td></td><td>a wimp</td></tr>
<tr><td>the whole 9 yards</td><td></td><td></td><td>direct</td></tr>
<tr><td>schmooze</td><td></td><td></td><td>go out of your way</td></tr>
<tr><td>get even</td><td></td><td></td><td>rub off on</td></tr>
<tr><td>rub the wrong way</td><td></td><td></td><td>have what it takes</td></tr>
<tr><td>up for</td><td></td><td></td><td>pick up</td></tr>
</table>

DIALOGUE MATCH: Speaker 1

- Read the parts of the dialogue below and choose one part to begin the conversation.
- Listen to Speaker 2 (page 152), who will respond to what you say.
- Number your part of the conversation 1, 3, 5

____Really? That's tough. Is there anything I can do to help you out?

____Hey, I thought I'd drop by to say hello and see how your trip was. But what's up? What's the matter?

____Yeah, I know what you mean. It's called Murphy's Law: If anything can go wrong, it will. Are you sure there isn't anything I can do? Do you want me to bring you something to eat?

TIC-TAC-TOE

Rules: Student X and Student O have 20 seconds to use the expressions correctly and meaningfully in a sentence. Student Referee will keep time, judge if the sentences are good, and mark the boxes with X or O. The first student to get three in a row wins the game!

buy some-thing	ask for it	baby-boomers
speak of the devil	gutsy	food for thought
a flake	make out	bent out of shape

yuppie	push your luck	cut corners
get away with	clueless	a catch-22
keep up on	funky	cut out for

a break	stay in touch	up front
Generation X	jazzed	guts
even out	catch on	straight

PASSWORD: Player 2

- Player 1 will read an expression to you. Find an expression on your list that has a similar meaning. Tell Player 1 (page 150), who will write it down.
- Take turns reading an expression and writing one down with Player 1 until your list is complete.

PLAYER 1		PLAYER 2	
Expression	Synonym	Expression	Synonym
	wine and dine	grow on	
	settle a score	straight	
	a hint	be up on	
	get on my nerves	a chicken	
	feel like	catch on	
	go all out	bend over backwards	

DIALOGUE MATCH: Speaker 2

- Speaker 1 (page 150) will begin the dialogue.
- Respond by choosing the most suitable response.
- Number your choices 2, 4, 6

____ Well, I'm in a bit of a funk. I spaced out and deleted the wrong file. It's going to take me a while to put it back together.

____ Oh, that would be great! I could go for a coffee and something sweet.

____ Not really, but thanks. I've got a lot to deal with right now. Ever since I got back from my business trip, I have a lot to catch up on. Now this happens!

Target pp. 40-46, 58-63	Expanded pp. 50-53, 67-71	In Context pp. 39-74
a drag	a burnout	a blast
a hassle	a drag	a bummer
a rain check	a hit (2)	a comeback
bite off more than you can chew	a pickup	a wimp
bring up	a setup	an update
burned out	bottom dollar	burn the candle at both ends
can't beat that	bottoms up	cheat on
click	burn out	check out
flip out	cover all the bases	cool
glitch	don't hold your breath	cut someone off
go out on	drag queen	drag queens
hit it off	drag something out of someone	easy-going
hold out	drag your feet	fill out
max out	flip someone off	folks
off base	flip your lid	fool yourself
off the hook	flip-flop	freak out
off the wall	give someone the finger	give up
on the level	held up	in the shop
pick up	hit	it's your call
play it by ear	hit it	keep up with
savvy	hit it big	laid off
set up	hit on	miss the boat
snooze	hit rock bottom	munch
tacky	hit someone up for something	off color
tailgate	hit the books	pick up scene
the ball's in your court	hit the jackpot	roll in
the bottomline	hit the sack	see the forest for the trees
twist my arm	hit the spot	shut eye
uptight	hold off	slopes
wisecracks	hold on	so far, so good
	hold out for	straight away
	hold the_____	tasteless
	hold your horses	the pits
	hook up with	the works
	hooked on	toilet-paper
	hooker	turn out
	in drag	weird
	pick up (6)	wishy-washy
	play hooky	
	play it cool	
	play it safe	
	play it straight	
	set up	
	the bottom of the barrel	
	touch base	
	wise up	
	wiseguy	

MEMORY JOLT

Work with one or two classmates. Look the chart below and see if you can remember other expressions which contain the key word.

Key Word	Related Expressions
hit	
play	
off	
hold	
bottom	
flip	

MIME: Student(s) 1

In a small group, choose from among the following expressions to act out. Cross off each one after your classmates answer. Student(s) 2 turn to page 155.

a rain check_____   bite off more than you can chew_____

twist one's arm_____   snooze_____

the ball's in your court_____   can't beat that_____

DOUBLE MEANING

Same expression, different meaning. Explain all the meanings of the expressions below.

tip	
hit	
pick up	
drag	
straight	
catch	
set up	
burn out	

MIME: Student(s) 2

Choose from among the following expressions to act out for Student Group 1. Check off the expression when they answer correctly.

bring up_____   tailgate_____

on the level_____   play it by ear_____

cover all the bases_____   don't hold your breath_____

DECODE

Decode the words below to find the missing letter. Use the hints! After you have the letters, figure out what the two expressions are and use them in a sentence.

1.

o o e n / __ / z	take a nap	=_____
g t t / __ / i p u	high strung	=_____
/ __ / s c k c r s e i w	joke	=_____
i k c c / __ /	hit it off	=_____
v / __ / y v a	know-how	=_____
t s / __ / p u	arrange	=_____

__ __ __ __ __ __

2.

n r i b / __ / p u	mention	=_____
y k c a / __ /	inappropriate	=_____
l d / __ / o o t u	wait	=_____
/ __ / e e v l n o e h t	honest	=_____
n r c k e / __ / h i a	guarantee	=_____
e h t k c s a / __ / t h	snooze	=_____

__ __ __ __ __ __

Write a sentence using the two expressions you have just decoded,

_____

Target pp. 76-81, 94-99	clean up one's act	In Context pp. 75-110
	cold blood	
a glutton for punishment	cold feet	a lift
a hunch	cold shoulder	a vicious circle
a klutz	cold war	add up
a rookie	come across	backfire
a tough act to follow	come off	bank on
call off	come on	beat-up
chip in	come on to	bid
cold turkey	come up	boo
come out smelling like a rose	count in	booked
come up with	count off	breakup
count on	count out	bribe
crooked	countdown	can't knock that
decent	don't count your chickens before	channel surf
fall back on	they hatch	count one's lucky stars
give it a shot	get one's act together	cover for
glued to	give my right arm	cup of tea
grin and bear it	knock it off	cut some slack
knock on wood	knock out	down to the wire
know the ropes	knock yourself out	end up
lighten up	learn the hard way	fall for something
on someone's case	left-wing	figure out
phony	make one's head spin	flicks
picky	miss one's calling	fridge
play hardball	Mr. Right	go through
red tape	off by a long shot	greedy
right up your alley	off someone's case	hang out
sleazy	play around	high and mighty
spin your wheels	play doctor	in the same boat
stick your neck out	play dumb	kick back
through the grapevine	play hard	knock down
	play hard to get	lotto
Expanded pp. 85-89, 103-108	play the game	new kid on the block
	put one's spin on	not miss a beat
a basketcase	red cent	on one's best behavior
a big shot	red-eye	oui
a case	right off the bat	promise the sun, moon, and stars
a chip off the old block	right on	push away
a chip on one's shoulder	right on the money	put up with
a knockout	right-wing	real
a redneck	roll out the red carpet	show one's true colors
a shot	school of hard knocks	snotty
a shot in the dark	spin out	sound advice
a shotgun wedding	stick out like a sore thumb	stand someone up
a spin	stick up for	straighten out
a spin doctor	sticky	take a long hard look
act all high and mighty	the chips are down	take someone's side
act out	the sticks	tequila
act up		the bar
call it a day		the ins and outs
call it a night		way to go
call it quits		workaholic
call off		
call one's bluff		
call someone on something		
call the shots		
can't knock that		
case in point		

Jeopardy

- Choose a category. Read the hints and see if you can name the expression.
- You have 10 seconds to name each expression. Write it down.
- If you can't think of the expression within 10 seconds, you lose your turn.

cold	shot	right	spin	stick
ruthless	give orders	perfect person	dizzy	touchy
conflict without fighting	way wrong	cut out for	fruitless effort	noticeable
give up	go for it	Republican	lose control	defend
afraid to get married	fat chance	great sacrifice	opinionated	the boondocks
snob	important person	straight away	ride	risk

ON THE PHONE

STUDENT 1: Begin the phone conversation. Number the lines 1, 3, 5...

_____OK. <u>Take it easy</u>. I'll <u>catch up with</u> you later. Bye!

_____That's right. They're always glad to take your money, but will <u>fight you tooth and nail</u> when you file a claim. They're a bunch of <u>crooks</u>! Oh well, how do you like your dentist?

_____Hello. I'm trying to <u>get a hold of</u> _____. Is he/she there?

_____What <u>a drag</u>! Three more times! That's going to <u>cost an arm and a leg</u>! How much will your insurance cover?

_____Yeah, sorry I didn't recognize your voice. I've been calling all over the place for you! You're <u>tough</u> to <u>get a hold of</u> today!

_____Well, you'd better start taking better care of your teeth otherwise you'll be <u>a glutton for punishment</u>! Good luck <u>playing hardball</u> with the insurance company!

STUDENT 2: You will receive a call from Student 1. Number your responses 2, 4, 6...

_____She's <u>decent</u>—a little <u>dry</u> on the personality, but she gets the job done. She's no <u>rookie</u>, I'll tell you that. She's <u>got her act together</u>.

_____It's me. Is that _____?

_____Thanks. I'll need it!. I'm going to <u>be on their case</u> if I have to <u>keep dragging information out of them</u>. By the time this is over, I'll have <u>learned the ropes</u> about dental insurance coverage. All these extra fees keep <u>coming out of the woodwork</u>, and I want to know what exactly they are for. Oh, I've got to take this call!

_____I know. I was at the dentist all morning, and my mouth is still sore. I've had to <u>learn the hard way</u> that I should have been flossing my teeth. I have to see the dentist at least three more times.

_____I'll <u>give you a ring</u> later this week! Bye

_____They'll cover some of it, but not all. I can't get a <u>straight</u> answer out of them about the actual cost. I have <u>a hunch</u> that I'm still going to <u>pay through the nose</u>. They <u>act all high and mighty</u> whenever I ask about my policy. It really <u>gets on my nerves</u>. <u>The bottom line</u> is that they're <u>just plain greedy</u>!

SUPERSTAR

For each point of the star, find the expressions which contain in, out, on, off, up.
Write them down and then explain what they mean.

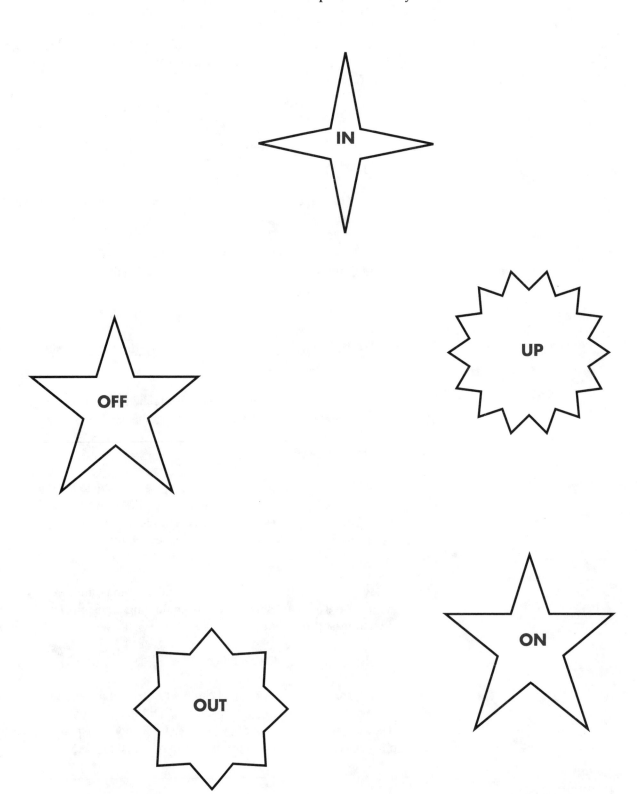

Target pp. 112-119, 132-138

a one-track mind
a taste of one's own medicine
add up
ahead of the game
an ivory tower
bail someone out
below the belt
bounce something off someone
burn one's bridges
carry weight
catch someone off guard
chew someone out
cranky
draw the line
geek
get up the nerve
gripe
lame
make a comeback
make ends meet
move on
on the back burner
practical joke
pull something off
pumped up
slick
the runaround
touchy
wacky
wipe out

Expanded pp. 123-128, 142-146

a bouncer
a one-liner
a piece of one's mind
add fuel to the fire
add insult to injury
add the finishing touches
at this stage of the game
back off
back streets
back up
back-to-back
belt it out
blow one's mind
bounce a check
bounce back
can't be touched
carry a torch
carry on (3)
carry one's own weight
carry the ball
catch one's breath
catch one's eye
catch someone red-handed

fair game
feed someone a line
get a move on
get back at
get back to
get on one's nerves
get the belt
have nerve
have nerves of steel
have one's mind in the gutter
hit a nerve
keep one's guard up
lay it one the line
let one's guard down
move in on
not touch with a 10-foot pole
on guard
on the line
on the move
online
out of line
out the moves on
pull a fast one
pull one's leg
pull oneself together
run around (2)
run around like a headless chicken
run around with
stab in the back
the game is up
the name of the game
tighten one's belt
touch on
touch up
touchy-feely
under one's belt

In Context pp. 111-148

a can of worms
a charmed life
a dweeb
a tight budget
back stab
bawl out
be up to something
beat around the bush
beg for
brag
busted
chutzpa
come through with flying colors
dry spell
fair game
fair share
fall apart
gender-bender
get ahead

get hammered
get ripped
give an inch, take a mile
go ahead
go full force
goof off
grand slam
grouchy
grumpy
handle
hardcore
have one's heart set on
hip
hysterical
I bet
in any way, shape, or form
jerk
let something slide
lose it
mess up
muster up
on edge
on one's own
party hard
pump iron
rumble
scheme
settle down
sleek
sore loser
spot
suit one's fancy
take one only so far
take something out on someone
take the bull by the horns
take with a grain of salt
tax breaks
tax-deferred
tekkies
the fine print
the good old boys
the guy thing
the silent treatment
this, that, and the other
top notch
top-notch
tough
toughen up
turn bright red
Uncle Sam
under the table
wasted
what you don't know can hurt you
what you don't know can't hurt you
whine

CROSSWORD PUZZLE

- Student 1: Read the Down clues to Student 2.
- Student 2: Write the Down answers.

DOWN

1. Another expression for give someone a taste of their own medicine? _ _ t _ _ _ _

2. How can you describe something that's unfair? _ _ _ _ w _ _ _ _ _ _ _

3. What's an expression for startle? _ _ _ _ _ _ _ f _ _ _ _ _

5. Someone who is strongly focused has a _ _ _ - _ _ a _ _ _ _ _ d.

6. If someone has a lot of importance, they _ _ _ _ y _ _ _ _ _ _

10. If you procrastinate, you put things on the _ _ _ _ _ u _ _ _ _

- Student 2: Read the Across clues to Student 1.
- Student 1: Write the Across answers.
- When both of you have finished, turn to page 163 to fill the puzzle in together.

ACROSS

4. An expression for someone who is forward thinking is _ _ _ _ _ _ _ _ _ _ _a _ _

6. If you have renewed success, you've made a _ _ _ _ _ _ _ k

7. Another expression to describe something that is sensitive is _ _ _ _ h _

8. Beat around the bush also means to give someone the _ _ _ a _ _ _ _ _

9. If you have a privileged life, you may be living in an _ _ _ _ _ _ _ w _ _

11. To set a limit, you have to _ r _ _ _ _ _ _ _ _ _

12. If you want someone's ideas, you might _ _ _ _ c _ something _ _ _ them.

13. To live within your income means that you can _ _ _ _ _ _ _ s _ _ _ _

TRIVIA

Find four expressions for each category.

"CRAZY"	1.	2.	3.	4.
"OUT OF TROUBLE"	1.	2.	3.	4.
"SOPHISTICATED"	1.	2.	3.	4.
"COMPUTER PERSON"	1.	2.	3.	4.
"DELICATE or SENSITIVE"	1.	2.	3.	4.
"VERY DRUNK"	1.	2.	3.	4.
"HONEST or FRANK"	1.	2.	3.	4.
"TOLERATE"	1.	2.	3.	4.
"STAY IN CONTACT"	1.	2.	3.	4.

CROSSWORD PUZZLE

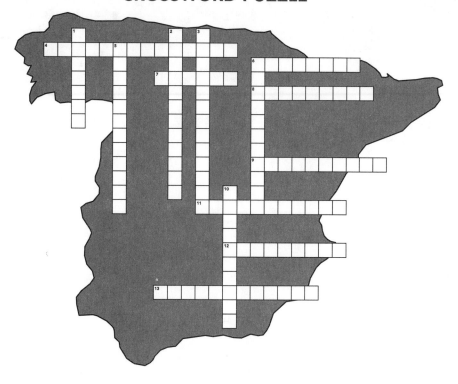

BINGO

Fill in the bingo boxes using the expressions from the list below. Write them in any order you please. Then play Bingo with your classmates. Take turns describing the expressions. The first person to get the expressions in a row horizontally, vertically, or diagonally wins. Do not look at each other's Bingo boxes!

add up	burn bridges	catch one's eye	fair game
bouncer	one-liner	hit a nerve	out of line
name of the game	touch on	the silent treatment	run errands
settle down	stand up to	toughen up	stab in the back
tighten one's belt	feed someone a line	blow one's mind	on the line
add insult to injury	carry the ball	belt it out	pull one's leg

		BINGO		

NEW EXPRESSION GUIDE

TV/Music/Radio/Movies/Friends/Acquaintances/Strangers/Newspapers/
Magazines/School/Beach/Restaurants/Clubs/Stores/Gym

**Use this Guide to find new expressions to record in your Expression Log.
Answer the following questions the best you can:**

1. WHAT_____
   What is the expression?

2. WHO_____
   *Who said it? (male, female, young, old...type of person—business person, student,
   worker, boss...)*

3. WHERE_____
   Where did you hear it? (place, location, time...)

4. HOW_____
   How was it said? (friendly, formally, angry, funny, neutral...)

5. MEANING_____
   What do you think it means? It's ok if you don't know, but ask someone!

6. SAMPLE SENTENCE_____
   _____

NEW EXPRESSIONS LIST

Use this page to keep track of all the new expressions that you record in your Expression Log.

Expression	Meaning
1.	
2.	
3.	
4.	
5.	
6.	
7.	
8.	
9.	
10.	
11.	
12.	
13.	
14.	
15.	
16.	
17.	
18.	
19.	
20.	
21.	
22.	
23.	
24.	
25.	
26.	
27.	
28.	
29.	
30.	

ANSWER KEY

CHAPTER 1

Part I

Student 1 - pp. 2-3

■ **Quick Fix**
1) 4
2) 5
3) 1
4) 2
5) 3

■ **Cloze It**
1) his break
2) the whole nine yards
3) catch on
4) straight
5) Don't push your luck

■ **Sense or Nonsense**
1) S
2) S
3) NS
4) NS
5) S

■ **Plug In**
1) straight
2) the break
3) pushing his luck
4) caught on to
5) the whole nine yards

Student 2 - pp. 4-5

■ **Quick Fix**
1) 3
2) 4
3) 2
4) 5
5) 1

■ **Cloze It**
1) wine and dine
2) is cut out for
3) guts
4) funky
5) doesn't buy

■ **Sense or Nonsense**
1) NS
2) NS
3) S
4) S
5) NS

■ **Plug In**
1) cut out for
2) guts
3) wined and dined
4) can't buy
5) funkiest

Student 3 - pp. 6-7

■ **Quick Fix**
1) 4
2) 1
3) 5
4) 3
5) 2

■ **Cloze It**
1) be jazzed
2) made out
3) yuppies
4) in a nutshell
5) you're asking for it

■ **Sense or Nonsense**
1) NS
2) S
3) S
4) NS
5) S

■ **Plug In**
1) How did you make out
2) jazzed
3) In a nutshell
4) a yuppie
5) asking for it

Part II

Student 1, p. 8

■ **Tell Me**
1) straight
2) push your luck getting...
3) the whole nine yards
4) give me a break
5) catch on

■ **Make This Make Sense (possible answers)**
1) ...HATE to go to...
2) It was a HUGE problem
3) ...:a gorgeous silver platter with our names engraved
4) ...will probably NEVER catch on big time in Brazil...
5) ...only 40 m.p.h...., so the cop...said,"Slow down next time"

Student 2, p. 9

■ **Tell Me**
1) don't buy it
2) guts
3) wine and dine
4) funky
5) cut out for

■ **Make This Make Sense (possible answers)**
1) ...chez moi (at my house!)
2) ...more conservatively...
3) ...DIDN'T buy...
4) ...should have...sure IS cut out for...because she has won
5) showed NO GUTS...

Student 3, p. 10

■ **Tell Me**
1) jazzed
2) yuppie
3) make out
4) in a nutshell
5) asking for it

■ **Make This Make Sense (possible answers)**
1) ...WILL BE asking for it...
2) must BE very jazzed...
3) ...to go into detail,...
4) ...FOLKS who care about a life philosophy
5) ...ALWAYS make out well

Part III

Find Out More, - pp. 12-14
1) Look, I have to be <u>honest</u> with you. Eduardo is <u>gay</u> and he hasn't told his parents because they are very <u>traditional</u>.
2) 1-c, 2-b, 3-a, 4-d
3) **(a)** play catch up
   (b) got caught
   (c) a catch

4) (a) bought into/bought
   (b) bought
   (c) buy

5) (a) gut, b
   (b) spilled his guts, d
   (c) a gut, a
   (d) gutsy, c

6) (a) funky/unappealing
   (b) am in a funk,funk/feeling blue, music

7) (a) read
   (b) neck, kiss heavily

CHAPTER 2

Part I

Student 1 - pp. 21-22

■ Quick Fix
1) 4
2) 5
3) 2
4) 1
5) 3

■ Cloze It
1) schmoozing
2) food for thought
3) tips
4) spaced out
5) has what it takes

■ Sense or Nonsense
1) NS
2) S
3) S
4) S
5) S

■ Plug In
1) food for thought
2) is spaced out
3) tips
4) has what it takes
5) schmoozes me

Student 2 - pp. 23-24

■ Quick Fix
1) 4
2) 1
3) 2
4) 5
5) 3

■ Cloze It
1) Speak of the devil!
2) cutting corners
3) a flake
4) 'll get even
5) to deal with

■ Sense or Nonsense
1) NS
2) NS
3) S
4) S
5) NS

■ Plug In
1) cut corners
2) 'll get even
3) Speak of the devil
4) to deal with
5) a flake

Student 3 - pp. 25-27

■ Quick Fix
1) 3
2) 5
3) 4
4) 1
5) 2

■ Cloze It
1) could get away with
2) keep/be up on
3) grows on
4) a wimp
5) to bend over backwards

■ Sense or Nonsense
1) NS
2) S
3) NS
4) NS
5) S

■ Plug In
1) got away with
2) a wimp
3) has been growing on me
4) so up on
5) bent over backwards

Part II

Student 1, p. 28

■ Tell Me
1) have what it takes
2) food for thought
3) spaced out
4) a tip
5) schmooze

■ Make This Make Sense (possible answers)
1) Yuppies are rarely...
2) ...Dr. White is not spaced out...
3) Most people don't have what it takes...
4) ...Now, I don't have to call...
5) ...the cop sometimes gets you...

Student 2, p. 29

■ Tell Me
1) get even
2) cut corners
3) speak of the devil
4) deal with
5) a flake

■ Make This Make Sense (possible answers)
1) and not restart at zero.
2) I was just thinking about you.
3) AOL will have to deal with...
4) ...such a brilliant businessperson.
5) revealed my secret

Student 3, p. 30

■ Tell Me
1) get away with
2) a wimp
3) bend over backwards
4) up on
5) grow on someone

■ Make This Make Sense (possible answers)
1) I will bend over backwards...
2) ...U.S., is very up on...
3) Walter isn't...difficult husband.
4) Rie enjoys...
5) ...a wimp to go...

Part III

Find Out More - pp. 32-33

1) a) lead
   b) source
   c) clue
   d) lead, source, clue, tip off
   e) tips, hints, clue
   f) tips
   g) tips, leads, sources
   h) tips

2) take out...on/couldn't take/doesn't have what it takes
3) to flake out/flaky/a flake
4) **a)** even the score
   b) even out
   c) even steven
5) d, c, e, b, a
6) b, e, a, f, d, c
7) answers will vary
8) **a)** is rubbing off on
   b) rubs someone the wrong way

CHAPTER 3

Part I

Student 1 - pp. 40-42
■ **Quick Fix**
1) 4
2) 5
3) 1
4) 3
5) 2

■ **Cloze It**
1) gone out on
2) uptight
3) play it by ear
4) a rain check
5) off the hook

■ **Sense or Nonsense**
1) NS
2) NS
3) S
4) NS
5) NS

■ **Plug In**
1) is off the hook
2) going out on
3) a rain check
4) Let's play it by ear
5) uptight

Student 2 - pp. 43-44
■ **Quick Fix**
1) 4
2) 5
3) 1
4) 2
5) 3

■ **Cloze It**
1) tailgater
2) off the wall
3) bit off more than he could chew
4) bring up
5) the wisecracks

■ **Sense or Nonsense**
1) NS
2) S
3) S/NS
4) NS
5) NS

■ **Plug In**
1) wisecracks
2) was brought up
3) tailgating me
4) off the wall
5) You've bitten off more than you can chew.

Student 3 - pp. 45-46
■ **Quick Fix**
1) 2
2) 4
3) 5
4) 1
5) 3

■ **Cloze It**
1) set him up
2) a drag
3) The ball's in her court.
4) on the level
5) burned out

■ **Sense or Nonsense**
1) S
2) S
3) NS
4) S
5) NS

■ **Plug In**
1) is on the level
2) The ball's in your court.
3) is burned out
4) set up
5) a drag

Part II

Student 1, p. 47
■ **Tell Me**
1) play it by ear
2) go out on
3) off the hook
4) uptight
5) a rain check

■ **Make This Make Sense (possible answers)**
1) I would hate to get...
2) ...she couldn't get off...
3) ...they didn't guarantee...
4) I always feel...
5) Mr. Clinton can't play it...

Student 2, p. 48
■ **Tell Me**
1) tailgater
2) wisecracks
3) bite off
4) off the wall
5) bring up

■ **Make This Make Sense (possible answers)**
1) ...usually don't watch....because they don't get...
2) ...so I don't have time...
3) It's bad....
4) Satomi enjoys...
5) ...in very big cities...

Student 3, p. 49
■ **Tell Me**
1) the ball's in your court
2) a drag
3) on the level
4) burned out
5) set up

■ **Make This Make Sense (possible answers)**
1) Don't be a wimp.
2) The Mafia isn't always...
3) ...is take a break.
4) I'm so bummed...I don't have any freetime...
5) ...usually try to set up...

Part III

Find Out More - pp. 50-52
1) **a)** be careful, prepared, don't take chances
   b) stay calm, keep your composure
   c) be honest, upfront, don't hide anything
2) **a)** are hooked on
   b) a hooker
   c) hook up with
   d) play hooky
3) **a)** serious
   b) serious
   c) joking
   d) serious

4) a) was set up
    b) setup
    c) set him up
    d) setup
5) a) 3
    b) 5
    c) 4
    d) 2
    e) 1
6) a) burned out
    b) was burned out
    c) a burnout

CHAPTER 4

Part I

Student 1 - pp. 58-59

■ **Quick Fix**
1) 3
2) 5
3) 2
4) 1
5) 4

■ **Cloze It**
1) twisted my arm
2) The bottom line
3) hold out
4) tacky
5) don't click

■ **Sense or Nonsense**
1) NS
2) NS
3) S
4) S
5) S

■ **Plug In**
1) hold out
2) twist my arm
3) me the bottom line
4) clicks
5) tackiest

Student 2 - pp. 60-61

■ **Quick Fix**
1) 2
2) 1
3) 4
4) 5
5) 3

■ **Cloze It**
1) maxed out
2) a hassle
3) off base
4) snoozing
5) are hitting it off

■ **Sense or Nonsense**
1) S
2) NS
3) S
4) S
5) NS

■ **Plug In**
1) hit it off
2) is maxed out
3) hassle
4) snoozing
5) were off base

Student 3 - pp. 62-63

■ **Quick Fix**
1) 4
2) 1
3) 5
4) 2
5) 3

■ **Cloze It**
1) can't be beat
2) savvy
3) picked up
4) flip
5) glitch

■ **Sense or Nonsense**
1) S
2) S
3) NS
4) S
5) NS

■ **Plug In**
1) have a glitch
2) can't be beat
3) is savvy about
4) flipped
5) pick up

Part II

Student 1, p. 64

■ **Tell Me**
1) hold out
2) tacky
3) twist my arm
4) the bottom line
5) click

■ **Make This Make Sense
(possible answers)**
1) ...as beautiful as possible
2) He twisted my arm...
3) I adore this guy...
4) ...is not open to interpretation
5) They didn't hold out at all.

Student 2, p. 65

■ **Tell Me**
1) a hassle
2) snooze
3) off base
4) maxed out
5) hit it off

■ **Make This Make Sense
(possible answers)**
1) ...I hope we see each other again soon.
2) I'm not wide awake at all...
3) It's such a hassle!
4) ...credit card isn't good...
5) ...cost him the election.

Student 3, p. 66

■ **Tell Me**
1) flip
2) savvy
3) glitch
4) pick up
5) can't be beat

■ **Make This Make Sense
(possible answers)**
1) ...view of the ocean...
2) ...so easy to teach...
3) Pele would make... because he is...
4) has some glitches...
5) I'm sure she'll flip...

Part III

Find Out More - pp. 67-69
1) c, d, a, b
    the bottom of the barrel, hit rock bottom, bottoms up
2) a) hold on   b) hold off
    c) held up   d) hold out for
    e) hold the onions   f) hold your horses
    g) don't hold your breath
3) a) check in on you   b) look at every aspect
4) a) hit it, hitting on   b) hit it big, hit the jackpot
    c) hit the sack, hit the books d) a hit, hit me up for
5) a) paid   b) truck
    c) bought   d) learn
    e) meet   f) get
    g) clean   h) give a ride

170   Join the Club - Level 2

6) a) give the finger, emotional - angry
    b) go insane, emotional - surprised
    c) decide, neutral
    d) reversal, emotional - surprised

CHAPTER 5

Part I

Student 1 - pp. 76-77

■ **Quick Fix**   ■ **Cloze It**
1) 5   1) came up with
2) 1   2) phony
3) 2   3) right up your alley
4) 3   4) a klutz
5) 4   5) learn the ropes

■ **Sense or Nonsense** ■ **Plug In**
1) NS   1) the ropes
2) NS   2) the phoniest
3) S   3) right up your alley
4) S   4) a klutz
5) S   5) come up with

Student 2 - pp. 78-79

■ **Quick Fix**   ■ **Cloze It**
1) 4   1) spin your wheels
2) 3   2) was glued to
3) 2   3) rookies
4) 5   4) went cold turkey
5) 1   5) picky

■ **Sense or Nonsense** ■ **Plug In**
1) S   1) a rookie
2) NS   2) picky
3) NS   3) spinning our wheels
4) NS   4) 'm glued to
5) S   5) went cold turkey

Student 3 - pp. 80-81

■ **Quick Fix**   ■ **Cloze It**
1) 4   1) grin and bear it
2) 5   2) red tape
3) 1   3) sleazy
4) 2   4) stick her neck out
5) 3   5) chipping in

■ **Sense or Nonsense** ■ **Plug In**
1) NS   1) sleazy
2) NS   2) chipped in
3) S   3) stuck my neck out
4) S   4) grin and bear it
5) NS   5) red tape

Part II

Student 1, p. 82

■ **Tell Me**   ■ **Make This Make Sense**
                           (possible answers)
1) a klutz   1) ...if they learn the
                            ropes...
2) right up your alley   2) ...definitely came up
                            with many....
3) phony   3) ...seemed so on the
                            level.
4) know the ropes   4) ...cold weather...
5) come up with   5) ...can't be a klutz.

Student 2, p. 83

■ **Tell Me**   ■ **Make This Make Sense**
                           (possible answers)
1) cold turkey   1) ...were so bored with...
2) glued to   2) ...will usually not try...
3) a rookie   3) ...stop smoking in
                            stages.
4) picky   4) ...would be an unwise
                            idea.
5) spin your wheels   5) ...a very dissatisfying
                            feeling of frustration.

Student 3, p. 84

■ **Tell Me**   ■ **Make This Make Sense**
                           (possible answers)
1) sleazy   1) You can seldom count
                            on...
2) stick your neck out   2) It was totally luxurious.
3) grin and bear it   3) ...was able to grin and
                            bear it...
4) red tape   4) ...is a headache.
5) chip in   5) ...have to stick their
                            necks out...

Part III

Find Out More - pp. 85-87
1) a) Come on - hurry up
    b) came across - discover
    c) came on to me - flirted
    d) come off it- stop being ridiculous
    e) came off - effect, impression
2) 1) d   2) e
    3) b   4) c
    5) f   6) a
3) a) a drive
    b) go around in circles, skid
    c) confused
    d) give one's opinion
4) a) cold war   b) in cold blood
    c) cold feet   d) cold shoulder
5) 1) c   2) a   3) d   4) b

6) **a)** resemble strongly
   b) quick to temper because of an inferiority complex
   c) difficult times, crises
7) **a)** stick out like a sore thumb
   b) the sticks
   c) sticky
   d) stick up for

CHAPTER 6

Part I

Student 1 - pp. 94-95

■ **Quick Fix**
1) 4
2) 5
3) 2
4) 1
5) 3

■ **Cloze It**
1) count on
2) a hunch
3) decent
4) heard through the grapevine
5) give snowboarding a shot

■ **Sense or Nonsense**
1) S
2) NS
3) S
4) S
5) NS

■ **Plug In**
1) a hunch
2) through the grapevine
3) count on
4) give wood carving a shot
5) decent

Student 2 - pp. 96-97

■ **Quick Fix**
1) 4
2) 1
3) 5
4) 2
5) 3

■ **Cloze It**
1) was called off
2) got on my case
3) a glutton for punishment
4) Knock on wood
5) play hardball

■ **Sense or Nonsense**
1) S
2) NS
3) NS
4) NS
5) S

■ **Plug In**
1) called off
2) on her husband's case
3) going to play hardball
4) a glutton for punishment
5) knock on wood

Student 3 - pp. 98-99

■ **Quick Fix**
1) 3
2) 1
3) 4
4) 5
5) 2

■ **Cloze It**
1) fall back on
2) lighten up
3) come out smelling like a rose
4) crooked
5) a tough act to follow

■ **Sense or Nonsense**
1) S
2) NS
3) S
4) S
5) NS

■ **Plug In**
1) came out smelling like a rose
2) fall back on
3) crooked
4) a tough act to follow
5) lighten up

Part II

Student 1, p. 100

■ **Tell Me**
1) through the grapevine
2) a hunch
3) give it a shot
4) decent
5) count on

■ **Make This Make Sense (possible answers)**
1) It's not sound advice
2) ...you shouldn't give windsurfing a shot
3) ...civil war can't count on their neighbors...
4) ...are cruel...
5) ...rarely follow their hunch.

Student 2, p. 101

■ **Tell Me**
1) play hardball
2) knock on wood
3) on your case
4) a glutton for punishment
5) call off

■ **Make This Make Sense (possible answers)**
1) It's really a drag...
2) ...you don't lead a balanced life.
3) ...who is not on my case about anything
4) ...something good to happen...
5) ...lawyers have to play hardball

Student 3, p. 102

■ **Tell Me**
1) lighten up
2) crooked
3) come out smelling like a rose
4) a tough act to follow
5) fall back on

■ **Make This Make Sense (possible answers)**
1) ...resign, didn't come out...
2) ...you have something to fall back on
3) ...shouldn't increase much.
4) ...make dangerous business partners.
5) ...because she was a tough act to follow.

Part III

Find Out More - pp. 103-106
1) c, a, d, e, b
2) **a)** a guess
   b) marriage due to pregnancy
   c) an amount measured to be drunk in one swallow
   d) very wrong, inaccurate, mistaken
   e) makes the decisions, has the authority
   f) boss, important person
3) d, e, a, b, c
4) b, d, e, a, f, c
5) **a)** missed your calling   **b)** call it a day
   c) called him on it/called his bluff
   d) called my bluff   **e)** calls the shots
6) **a)** plays hard to get - show little or no interest
   b) play the game - follow the unspoken rules as expected
   c) played around, learned the hard way - cheat on, learn through mistakes
   d) played hard - have fun being very active
   e) played dumb - pretend not to have information or know anything
   f) play doctor, play doctor - pretend to be a doctor
7) e, a, b, c, d

CHAPTER 7

Part I

Student 1 - pp. 113-114

■ **Quick Fix**
1) 3
2) 4
3) 5
4) 1
5) 2

■ **Cloze It**
1) give her a taste of her own medicine
2) practical joke
3) burn your bridges
4) touchy
5) pulled off

■ **Sense or Nonsense**
1) NS
2) S
3) S
4) S
5) S

■ **Plug In**
1) a practical joke
2) pulled it off
3) touchy
4) a taste of your own medicine
5) burned their bridges

Student 2 - pp. 115-117

■ **Quick Fix**
1) 2
2) 5
3) 4
4) 1
5) 3

■ **Cloze It**
1) draw the line
2) cranky
3) will bail her out
4) pumped up
5) giving me the runaround

■ **Sense or Nonsense**
1) NS
2) NS
3) S
4) NS
5) S

■ **Plug In**
1) give their clients the runaround
2) cranky
3) pumped up
4) draw the line
5) bail you out

Student 3 - pp. 118-119

■ **Quick Fix**
1) 3
2) 4
3) 1
4) 5
5) 2

■ **Cloze It**
1) carry any weight
2) a one-track mind
3) caught me off guard
4) wiped out
5) is always griping

■ **Sense or Nonsense**
1) S
2) S
3) S
4) S
5) S

■ **Plug In**
1) was caught off guard
2) gripe
3) Sean carries weight
4) has a one-track mind
5) wiped out

Part II

Student 1, p. 120

■ **Tell Me**
1) touchy
2) pull something off
3) give someone a taste up...
4) burn one's bridges
5) practical joke

■ **Make This Make Sense (possible answers)**
1) ...It's not easy...
2) ...by doing exactly what I...
3) ...jokes usually crack of their own medicine
4) ...the swimmer pulled off setting...
5) ...so I'm not going to...

Student 2, p. 121

■ **Tell Me**
1) bail someone out
2) pumped up
3) the runaround
4) cranky
5) draw the line

■ **Make This Make Sense (possible answers)**
1) ...you have to draw the line...
2) ...feel energetic...
3) ...be tough to have...
4) ...I know I can't trust...
5) Being happy is...

Student 3, p. 122

■ **Tell Me**
1) catch someone off guard
2) gripe
3) carry weight
4) wiped out
5) a one-track mind

■ **Make This Make Sense (possible answers)**
1) ...may be wiped out...
2) ...a lousy conversationalist.
3) ...you have to know...
4) ...is very annoying.
5) It's bad to be...

Part III

Find Out More - pp. 123-126

1) **a)** can't be touched **b)** touched on
   c) touched up
   d) wouldn't touch it with a ten-foot pole
   e) touchie-feely
2) **a)** calm down **b)** kidding
   c) deceive to gain advantage
3) c, a, d, b
4) **a)** lay it on the line **b)** line
   c) online **d)** out of line
   e) one-liners **f)** fed me a line
   g) laid her life on the line
5) d, c, e, f, a, b
6) **a)** give him a piece of my mind
   b) blows my mind **c)** his mind in the gutter
7) c, f, a, e, b, d

CHAPTER 8

Part I

Student 1 - pp. 132-134

Quick Fix   Cloze It
1) 3   1) got up the nerve
2) 5   2) slick
3) 1   3) made a comeback
4) 2   4) on the back burner
5) 4   5) chew out

■ **Sense or Nonsense**   ■ **Plug In**
1) T   1) chewed me out
2) F   2) slick
3) F   3) put it on the back
                        burner
4) T   4) got up the nerve
5) T   5) make a comeback

Student 2 - pp. 135-136
■ **Quick Fix**   ■ **Cloze It**
1) 3   1) lame
2) 5   2) the ivory tower, an
                        ivory tower existence
3) 1   3) to make ends meet
4) 2   4) to move on
5) 4   5) hit below the belt

■ **Sense or Nonsense**   ■ **Plug In**
1) T   1) lives in an ivory tower
2) F   2) lame
3) F   3) move on
4) T   4) make ends meet
5) F   5) hit below the belt

Student 3 - pp. 137-138
■ **Quick Fix**   ■ **Cloze It**
1) 5   1) bounce an idea off you
2) 1   2) wacky
3) 2   3) adds up
4) 3   4) a geek
5) 4   5) stay ahead of the game

■ **Sense or Nonsense**   ■ **Plug In**
1) T   1) bounce this idea off you
2) T   2) add up to
3) T   3) a geek
4) F   4) wacky
5) T   5) ahead of the game

Part II

Student 1, p. 139
■ **Tell Me**   ■ **Make This Make Sense**
                                (possible answers)
1) put it on the back   1) It's not alright if...
   burner
2) make a comeback   2) ...very clumsy.
3) chew out   3) If you can get up...
4) slick   4) ...must be very
                               satisfying.
5) get up the nerve   5) I do mind being...

Student 2, p. 140
■ **Tell Me**   ■ **Make This Make Sense**
                                (possible answers)
1) lame   1) ...probably not want to
                               live...
2) make ends meet   2) ...one of the best gifts...
3) ivory tower   3) It's uncomfortable to get
                               hit...
4) below the belt   4) ...and didn't get back
                               together...
5) move on   5) ...is a lousy way...

Student 3, p. 141
■ **Tell Me**   ■ **Make This Make Sense**
                                (possible answers)
1) geek   1) ...for an average type of
                               person.
2) add up   2) I don't like it when...
3) bounce something off   3) It's tough to...
   someone
4) ahead of the game   4) Geeks make crummy...
5) wacky   5) ...by putting nothing...

Part III

1) a) alleys, side streets, short cuts
    b) stop pressuring
    c) alternative   d) deceived; get even
    e) non-stop, contact
2) a) nerves of steel   b) hit a nerve
    c) gets on my nerves   d) has a lot of nerve
3) a) belt it out   b) under my belt
    c) tighten your belt   d) get the belt
4) b, c, d, a

5) a) my check bounced - bank returned check due to insufficient funds
    b) bounced back - recovered quickly
    c) the bouncer - person employed to handle people who get out of line
6) a) add the finishing touches
    b) add fuel to the fire
    c) add insult to injury
7) a) the name of the game
    b) At this stage of the game
    c) fair game
    d) the game is up

REVIEW— CHAPTERS 1 and 2, pp. 149-152

Password: Players 1 and 2 (p. 150 and 152)

Expression	Synonym	Expression	Synonym
schmooze	wine and dine	grow on	rub off on
get even	settle a score	straight	direct
a tip	a hint	be up on	have what it takes
rub the wrong way	get on my nerves	a chicken	a wimp
up for	feel like	catch on	pick up
the whole nine yards	go all out	bend over backwards	go out of your way

Dialogue Match: Speaker 1: (p. 150) 3, 1, 5   **Speaker 2:** (p. 152) 2, 6, 4

REVIEW— CHAPTERS 3 and 4, pp. 153-156

Memory Jolt, p. 154

Key Word: **Related Expressions**

hit   a hit, hit it, hit it big, hit on, hit rock bottom, hit someone up, hit it off, hit the jackpot/bottle/books/sack/

play   play it by ear, play hooky, play it straight/cool/safe

off   laid off, off base, off the hook, off the wall, hold off

hold   hold off/out/out for/on/in/up, hold your horses, hold the_____

bottom   hit rock bottom, the bottom line, bottom dollar, bottoms up

flip   flip, flip out, flip off, flip -flop, flip someone out, flippy, flip your lid...

Double Meaning, p. 155

tip: a hint, advice, leave money

hit: a puff, a drag, a big success, strike

pick up: pay for, buy, clean up, learn, a truck, an easy person to meet, retrieve, make advances...

drag: a puff, a hit, a bummer, an annoying situation, move slowly

straight: honest, not gay, traditional, no longer criminal

catch: a drawback, a good mate

set up: deal dishonestly, frame, arrange, start, falsely accuse, make look guilty

burn out: exhaust, use up, stop functioning, expire

Decode, p. 156
1. S -snooze, H -uptight, A -wisecracks, L click, S -savvy, E set up = hassle
2. G -bring up, T -tacky, H -hold out, L -on the level, C -raincheck, I -hit the sack = glitch

REVIEW— CHAPTERS 5 and 6, pp. 157-160

Jeopardy, p. 158

cold: in cold blood, the cold war, cold turkey, cold feet, cold shoulder

shots: call the shots, off by a long shot, give it a shot, a shot in the dark, a big shot

right: Mr. Right, right up your alley, right-winged, give my right arm, right off the bat

spin: make your head spin, spin your wheels, spin out, spin doctor, a spin

stick: sticky, stick out like a sore thumb, stick up for, the sticks, stick your neck out

On The Phone, p. 159

Student 1: 11, 7, 1, 5, 3, 9   **Student 2:** 8, 2, 10, 4, 12, 6

Superstar, p. 160

in: chip-count-come in, case in point

off: call-come-count off, knock it off, right off the bat

on: come on, come on to, right on, fall back on, knock on wood

out: figure-roll-spin-knock-count-act-come-hang out

up: pick-beat-end-clean-come-act-lighten-break-catch-give-take-set-up, stick up for, up for, up on, up front...

REVIEW—CHAPTERS 7 and 8, pp. 161-164

Crossword Puzzle, p. 162

Down:

1. get even
2. below the belt
3. catch off guard
5. one track mind
6. carry weight
10. back burner

Across:

4. ahead of the game
6. comeback
7. touchy
8. runaround
9. ivory tower
11. draw the line
12. bounce off
13. make ends meet

Trivia, p. 163

crazy: wacky, zany, off the wall, loopy, out there, nuts, hysterical, lose it...

out of trouble: off the hook, not in hot water, get away with, pull off, bail out

sophisticated: savvy, slick, hip, up on, have what it takes...

computer person: nerd, geek, dweeb, freak, egghead, tekkie...

delicate or sensitive: touchy, sticky, uptight, high strung, on edge, bent out of shape...

very drunk: hammered, ripped, wasted, hit the bars, hit the bottle...

honest/frank: the bottom line, straight, on the level, up front, lay it on the line, put your cards on the table...

tolerate: put up with, grin and bear it, hold out, stick it out

moody: cranky, grumpy, grouchy, touchy, bent out of shape, can't stand, fed up with, sick of, have had it...

complain: rub the wrong way, gripe, moan, hassle, whine, bent out of shape, fed up with, have had it...

funny: hysterical, crack up, one-liner, practical joke, stunt, prank...

stay in contact: keep in touch, touch base, get back to, catch you later, catch up with, ring...

TRANSCRIPTS: TUNE IN

CHAPTER 1, p. 16

Possible key words and phrases are in bold.

1) Gary has always had **a natural talent** and **interest** for fixing things. When he was a kid, he loved to build model cars and airplanes. When he was a teenager, he spent a lot of time taking apart motors just to see how things work. His job selling computers is **perfect for him**. That is why **he is so good at it**. (be cut out for)

2) It took **a lot of time, effort, planning and courage,** but Takaya **decided** to completely **change her life** and move to the States. She was **scared, but** she knew it was the right thing to do. She **feels** really **proud** of herself now. (guts)

3) Paul **picks up** languages so **quickly** that it's amazing! He's a great language learner because he's not afraid to make mistakes. He knows how to listen, he knows how to study, and he makes friends easily with native speakers. (catch on)

4) Some people think that if you work hard and are determined to do what you know you enjoy doing and are good at, a great **opportunity** will open up to you. (a break)

5) We had a very **successful** year. Everybody worked really hard and **made the business grow**! So for the first time, we are able to **offer** all the employees **a bonus**. We definitely want to keep everyone here happy! (make out)

6) Even though Stacy has a lot of credit card **debt**, she still **doesn't think twice** about buying **new expensive clothes**. She even told me the other day she's thinking about leasing a **brand new Audi Quattro**. (yuppie)

7) Maggie **couldn't believe** the guy her sister chose to marry because all the stories about his past didn't add up. She kept telling her to wait awhile longer—that there was no hurry to get married! Sure enough, after they got married, her sister **found out** that he had been married before and had two children! (buy something)

8) Last night I was going to watch a video, but on channel 3 there was an infomercial about the biggest hits of **rock and roll** from the **1960's - 1990's**. **I knew almost every song**, so I couldn't resist. I called the 800 number and ordered the collection. I think **a lot of people** must have done the same. (baby boomer)

9) What a **dilemma**! We can't afford to put her in the hospital and we can't take care of her properly at home. We're going to have to come up with some solution for this difficult situation. (catch-22)

10) Dorothy and Jerry are **really going all out** for their vacation to Alaska. They're taking a luxury cruise up there, during which they'll be able to see the **fantastic** killer whales. Then they're renting a **gorgeous** cabin in the national park where they'll be able to take some **outstanding** pictures of the Northern Lights. (the whole nine yards)

11) Let me **understand this clearly**: Your father won't let you go camping with us because he thinks we might do something he wouldn't approve of? He sounds really **conservative**. Did you tell him that Julie and Nancy are going too? (get something straight, be straight).

12) We had the worst flight of our life, but **the long and short of it** is that we got back safely and none of our bags are missing! We are just so glad to be home! (in a nutshell)

13) Jose is **ecstatic** about his new job. He is doing exactly what he wants to do AND he's making better money. All his hard work, studies, and effort have really paid off! Now he should have no problem facing the Monday through Friday routine. He's really **thrilled**! (be jazzed)

14) I really liked that movie. It was **right on** even though it was **bizarre**. It took me a while to **figure out** what was going on, but after that one scene, I finally **got it**. (funky, catch on)

15) **Taking me out and treating me to a good time** isn't the way to get information out of me. **You're lucky I'm telling you this**, because if you ask the wrong person, **you'll probably lose your business**. (wine and dine, asking for it, push your luck)

CHAPTER 2, p. 36

1) When Martin Luther King Jr. gave his famous "I Have a Dream" speech at the Washington Memorial in 1963, he gave the American people plenty of **food for thought** regarding civil rights and race relations. (yes—this is one of the most famous speeches of the 20th century)

2) I was able to move to my new place because of all the help Stefano gave me. He really bent over backwards to help me move because he is such **a flake**. (no—a flake is usually unreliable and probably wouldn't help someone out this way)

3) Whenever I feel **spaced out**, I love to work a lot because I can concentrate so clearly, find a lot of **corners to cut**, and get so much done. (no—if you're spaced out, it's difficult to concentrate and you usually can't cut any corners either)

4) Thanks a lot for your **tip** about purchasing the exercise bike on the Web. I got it for $100.00 less than the cheapest price I'd found in the stores! (yes—a tip is helpful and useful information)

5) We recently made changes in our program to make it better. Because of these changes, there are more details and meetings to **deal with** to make sure that everything is going as smoothly as possible. (yes—changes at work usually bring about more things to do—deal with, especially at the beginning)

6) Barbara Streisand and her husband James Brolin were being followed by paparazzi who were taking pictures of them while they were trying to enjoy their private time. So they went straight to the police to make sure that the paparazzi wouldn't **get away with** invading their privacy. (yes—the police are supposed to take action if someone is being followed)

7) Mary is such a pleasant person to work with because she usually **takes her frustrations out on** us by either not talking to us or by barking orders at us. (no—someone who takes out their frustrations on you is not a pleasant person to be around)

8) What's the **big deal** if we arrive at the party a few minutes late? It's not a formal dinner party or anything like that. I don't think we'll **rub anyone the wrong way** if we are a few minutes late, so let's not rush. (yes—usually it's ok to be a little late to casual parties in the U.S.)

9) Chris said he'd pay us $50.00 an hour plus **tips**, so we should have gotten about $500.00. But when the check arrived, we were short about $200.00 each. So we called to let him know that we **were even**. (no—he still owes some money)

10) You'll never guess who I ran into the other day at the store...you won't believe me even if I tell you, but I swear I saw Jim Smith. **Speak of the devil**...We didn't recognize each other at first...(no—you would have to have been thinking about Jim beforehand)

11) Henry said he feels like **a wimp** at work because it's so hard to **keep up on** all the latest technology he has to learn. He doesn't think he **has what it takes** to work in the high tech industry. (yes—if he feels like a wimp at work, he doesn't think he is capable of being in that field)

12) Curt seems to be **growing on** the boss more and more each week. All his **schmoozing** may lead him to a promotion soon. (yes—a natural outcome of effective schmoozing could be a promotion)

CHAPTER 3 - p. 54

1) Rita was <u>a big disappointment</u> to go on vacation with because she wanted to plan everything—she <u>wouldn't do anything spontaneously</u> because she's so <u>high-strung</u>. (serious: a drag, play it by ear, uptight)

2) Look, I have to be <u>straight</u> with you. Sales have been down for two years now. No one is going to get a bonus this year, and worst of all, 10% of the jobs here are going to be cut. <u>It's your choice</u>, but I'd <u>start arranging</u> some job interviews if I were you. (serious: on the level-level with, the ball's in your court, set up)

3) That play we saw at the theater last night was <u>crazy</u>! We'd never seen anything like it before. The actors were improvising and they kept <u>mentioning</u> all these <u>witty remarks</u>. It was hysterical. You should see it! (positive: off the wall, bring up, wisecracks)

4) I'm really getting <u>fed up with</u> the way you drive! Would you <u>get off that guy's bumper</u> and slow down please! You'd better <u>be careful</u>! What is your big hurry? (serious: burned out, tailgate, play it safe)

5) I'm glad you <u>mentioned</u> lunch because you just reminded me that I have a dentist appointment later this afternoon, so I'll have to <u>catch you another time</u>. (neutral: bring up, a rain check)

6) Dan had better <u>watch out</u>. He's <u>cheating on</u> his wife AND his girlfriend. He's really <u>asking for it</u>. I'm sure he won't be able to <u>get away with</u> this much longer. (serious: wise up, go out on, bite off more than he can chew, off the hook)

7) Oh—this is incredible! How did you make this? I <u>could eat this every day and never get sick of it</u>! Come on—tell me—what's your secret? Oh come on—are you going to <u>make me beg you for it</u>? (positive: be hooked on, drag it out of you)

8) I <u>don't want to take any chances</u> because I've never bought such a high-tech sound system before, so would you please help me <u>put it together</u> so that the speakers <u>don't blow out</u>. (neutral: play it safe, set up, go out on)

9) Finally—you're home! <u>You'd better tell me</u> where you've been. Ugh, you smell like smoke! Don't tell me you took <u>a puff</u> on one of Nick's cigars? <u>I'm getting</u>

really <u>sick and tired</u> of wondering where you are! (serious: play it straight, a drag, burned out)

10) I can't <u>procrastinate</u>—I have to do it now, not later. I'm really <u>burning the candle at both ends</u>, but I want to make the deadline. I'd better <u>stay calm</u> and just keep working until I finish! (serious: drag my feet, bite off more than I can chew, play it cool)

CHAPTER 4, p. 72

1) We just had a **top of the line** computer system installed in our new offices. It is absolutely amazing—extremely expensive but worth every cent! With all the money we spent, there shouldn't be any **defects**, but you never know with computers. If there are, the technical support team will take care of them right away. It's under the service contract. (can't be beat, glitches)

2) We began investigating computer systems about a year ago. We gathered a ton of information and consulted with several companies, and I'm really glad that we were able to **withstand** the temptation of buying that system with all the fancy extras that we really didn't need. We got exactly what we need for our business. That first computer consulting company tried to **win us over** by telling us we needed all the extras that we really didn't. It is so important to have a clear understanding of what you need. They really got on my nerves after awhile! (hold out for, twist our arm)

3) In fact, the price quotes that they gave us were really **out of line** with what other companies offered. It is a good thing we checked out several other companies and that we held out for a company that could be on the level with us. We realized that the first company is new, but it was clear they weren't very **knowledgeable** or refined when it comes to understanding how to cut a deal with a customer. (off base, savvy)

4) What's more, that company had **no class**! They were so unprofessional that they actually got angry with us for going with another vendor even though we kept telling them what our needs were. **The fact of the matter** is that company is only interested in making a quick profit as opposed to establishing a good customer relationship. In the long run, service counts more. They'll learn the hard way. I'm sure they won't be able to stay in business very long because there is too much competition. (tacky, the bottom line)

5) Learning a new computer system is **a huge bother** for some people, but the more exposure you have, the more likely you'll be able to **acquire** a sense of how the system works. The important thing is not to feel too

exasperated when you don't understand how to do something right away. It takes some patience! (hassle, pick up, flip out)

6) When you're learning a new computer application, be sure you know when you reach your limit so that you don't get information **overload**! I always begin to feel **drowsy** when this happens. I need to take a break for a while so that the information can sink into my brain. (max out, snooze)

7) I always work better after a short break. Things **fit together** more clearly. When this happens, I **get along really well** with all my co-workers because I can share what I know with a lot more enthusiasm and patience. I'm probably much easier to work with too because I feel like I'm not **wasting my time** endlessly on the computer. I don't feel so frustrated with all the information! (click, hit it off, spin my wheels)

CHAPTER 5, p. 90

1) Have you ever had a million things to do but not enough time to finish? What would you do in that case? Would you ask someone to help you out or would you find a solution to lighten your load? (chip in, spin your wheels, come up with, grin and bear it)

2) Can you think of a time when you went out of your way to help someone out even though it was risky for you? How did it turn out? Has someone ever gone out of their way for you? (stick your neck out)

3) If you could give up something immediately, what would it be? Or, is there someone you know who should quit doing something? (cold turkey)

4) Describe a time when you were new at something and you had to figure out all of the ways things were expected to be done. (rookie, learn the ropes)

5) What do you think about people who are very particular about the food they eat? Have you ever gone to a nice restaurant with such a person? Did they send the food back to the kitchen? (picky, grin and bear it)

6) Is there anyone in your family that you resemble, either a physical resemblance or a character trait? Or do you know of anyone who is just like someone in their family for the same reasons? (a chip off the old block)

7) Describe an area in your country or one that you have visited where the people have a very closed and narrow-minded mentality. Why do you think they are like that? Is it because they live in an isolated region, because they are just ignorant, or because they have a very conservative government? (redneck, the sticks, right-winged)

8) Tell us about a time when you were completely transfixed by something, for example, a movie, a book, a story, etc. Why do you think you were so taken with it? Why did it seem to suit you? (be glued to, right up your alley)

9) Have you ever got caught up in bureaucratic procedure? What were the circumstances? How did you figure out what to do? How long did everything take? Did you ever get fed up with it or express exasperation? (red tape, come on, come off it)

10) When someone seems as though they aren't for real, that they aren't being straight with you, or that they are just putting on airs trying to impress you, what do you do? Would you turn your nose up to them or would you tolerate the situation until you could make a graceful exit? (phony, sleazy, cold shoulder, grin and bear it)

CHAPTER 6, p. 109 (possible responses)

1) The government told the student demonstrators that if they protested against the trade limitations, the school administrators would expel all of them from school. Many people thought the response of the government was too extreme, and that they should listen to what the students had to say by allowing them to voice their opinions. It is, after all, supposed to be a free country where people have freedom of speech! (play hardball, lighten up)

2) Due to the threat of being expelled from school, the student demonstration was postponed until the students could find a way to get their message heard. They knew they could depend on the university radio station to support their cause. If they couldn't do it directly, they could at least get their message across through the radio waves in the hopes that people would tune in and listen to what they had to say. (call off, through the grapevine, count on)

3) Fortunately, one well-known talk radio host heard about the problems the students were having. He took their side and offered to let them air their views on his talk show just in case the school authorities gave the campus radio station a hard time about airing the voices of the students. Naturally, the students were jazzed to have such a popular radio personality interested in and supportive of their cause. (on one's case, fall back on)

4) The day arrived when the students were able to voice their opinion on both the campus radio station and on the popular radio talk show. Both talk show hosts had a feeling that most people would agree with the students, so they arranged for there to be open lines for people to call into the stations and have a discussion with the students. The show was so popular that more and more people called in to request further information, so they decided to air the students regularly twice a week. (a hunch, a tough act to follow)

5) Finally, one school authority, Mr. Daner, a university administrator who had originally threatened to expel the students, listened to one of the radio shows. After thinking about their points, he decided to support the students in their cause to negotiate with the government for alternative trade limitations. Because of his support, the university ended up not looking like the bad guy as they were in the beginning. (give them a shot, decent, come out smelling like a rose)

6) Yet not all the university authorities agreed with Mr. Daner. In fact, they indirectly threatened to make his life miserable if he continued to support the students. However, it was clear that public opinion sympathized with the cause of the students, as did most small business owners. Mr. Daner felt very grateful that perhaps public opinion would continue to have a strong influence and that some compromise could be made between the government, the students and the small business owners. Mr. Daner wanted to do the right thing, but he also didn't want to be a martyr and have his career destroyed. (crooked, knock on wood, a glutton for punishment)

7) Finally, after several news stories and weeks of radio shows, the students, the small business owners, Mr. Daner and the government officials all got together for a live televised debate. Each side had spent a considerable amount of time preparing for the debate. The government officials had to look as though they were still in control of the situation. The students had to be well prepared to debate the government and make sure that they could justify their claims as to why trade limitations had to be so strict. Were they truly interested in the will of the people, or were they motivated by money and power? (get it together, call the shots, call someone's bluff)

CHAPTER 7, p. 129

1) You have to be a lawyer to be able to understand most legal documents because of all the legalese written in (fine print).

2) Another way to say that you are totally jazzed and excited about something is (pumped up).

3) He was so embarrassed because he didn't know I could see him drinking directly from the milk carton. I (caught him off guard).

4) No one can make pasta better than Guilio. Believe me, his ravioli is the best. It (can't be touched).

5) Last year Edna got away with being late to work and she still got the same raise as everyone else, but this year she won't be able to (pull it off).

6) The floods in Mozambique completely destroyed the food supply of the whole country. Every crop got completely (wiped out).

7) Another way to say that you're sick and tired of something or that you've had it is (fed up with).

8) Many people wait until the last possible moment to pay their bills without getting a late fee. They want to hold on to their money as long as possible, so they (put it off).

9) The quarter is almost over, and the students are really ready for a break, but they have to finish, so they'll (stick it out).

10) Ugh! That cheese smells disgusting. Get it away from me. I wouldn't (touch it with a ten-foot pole).

11) Thanks for helping me out again and covering for me at work. This was a tough time, but you (bailed me out).

12) Another expression for get even or even the score is to give someone (a taste of their own medicine).

13) My brother loves to play tricks on his neighbors. He plans them out carefully and then video tapes them. Some people get a little mad, but usually they enjoy his (practical jokes).

14) A lot of fans started to go crazy at the soccer match. They started throwing bottles and swearing at each other. Soon the police had to come because things (got out of hand).

15) If you promise to keep a secret, you can say that (your lips are sealed).

16) Grumpy and grouchy are synonyms for (cranky).

17) Another way to say that you're going to be straight with someone and give them the bottom line is to (lay it on the line).

18) Sometimes people schmooze other people by telling them something to flatter them. They (feed them a line).

19) If someone starts to talk about something you feel sensitive about, you might become a little (touchy).

20) If someone constantly tries to take advantage of you, you'd better (stand up to them/draw the line).

21) We wanted to buy new furniture, but we had already paid cash for a new car. We didn't want to max out our credit cards, so we set our limits and (drew the line).

22) That was one of the best movies I have ever seen. The special effects were incredible. They really (blew my mind).

23) Another way to say you like to socialize and hang out with is to (run around with).

24) A good way to learn about computers is to play around on them if you have extra time. Sometimes you can discover new tricks by (goofing off).

25) If you're disappointed with someone you care about, it may be tough, but it's a good idea to give them (a piece of your mind).

26) If you have cosmetic surgery, there is no turning back. You'll never look the same again. You have to be ready to (burn your bridges).

27) Another word which means to complain or whine is (gripe).

28) Fred wants to hit the casinos every chance he gets. I think he's becoming addicted to gambling because of his (one-track mind).

29) How on earth did you plan this surprise party without my finding out? You all really (pulled a fast one).

30) In most companies, it's the Chief Executive Officer who (carries the weight).

31) Marcia is so gullible. She'll believe almost anything anyone tells her. She's always (falling for something).

32) Another way to say someone is misbehaving or is being inappropriate is to say they are (out of line).

CHAPTER 8, p. 147 (possible answers)

1) The practical joke we played on April Fool's Day went a little too far. We planned it for months, and we got up the nerve to pull it off, but we didn't mean to rub anyone the wrong way. I hope they didn't take it the wrong way. It sure made us laugh though! (get on one's nerves, hit below the belt, add insult to injury, crack up)

2) I need to learn more about web publishing because next year I'm going to be on a committee to update our web site. I want to be up on what's happening and get it together so that I will understand the latest technology. I don't want to put this off. It has to be a priority. (ahead of the game, slick, the back burner)

3) I need to get your input. You might think some of what I have to say is crazy, but hear me out. What do you think if we begin by discussing our options? That way we can realistically analyze the possible outcomes of our choices. We can see which ones make the most sense because we have to make some changes. That is where my wild and unconventional ideas come in. Let's be creative! (bounce something off someone, add up, move on, wacky)

4) Madonna may be leading a charmed life now, but it wasn't always that way for her. She left home when she was only 19 years old and moved to New York City with only $30.00 in her pocket. It was very challenging for her to survive, but she has always had a one-track mind about her work. She has also been very gutsy. Critics always say she is all washed up, but she always pumps out hit after hit after hit. These are just a few reasons she continues to be such a phenomenal success. (an ivory tower, make ends meet, nerves of steel, make a comeback)

5) Tom bugged everyone in the office today because he always has to show off how much more he knows about computers than everyone else. Derrick finally put him in his place by telling him how annoying it was of him to always compete with other people for no real reason. He doesn't know when enough is enough. (hit a nerve, get on one's nerves, geek, stand up to, lame, draw the line)

INDEX - GLOSSARY

Expression	Chapter	Page	Meaning
can't see the forest...**:VP	4	70	get caught up in details
carry a torch*:VP	7	125	unrequited feelings of affection
carry on*:PV	7	125	behave in a silly way
carry on*:PV	7	125	exaggerate, be melodramatic
carry on*:PV	7	125	move on, go forward
carry one's (own) weight*:VP	7	125	be responsible for yourself
carry the ball*:VP	7	125	capable of doing difficult tasks
carry weight:VP	7	118	be influential, important
case in point*:NP	6	104	example, illustration
case*:NP	6	104	legal proceeding, paperwork
catch on:PV	1	2	come to understand
catch one's breath*:VP	7	125	relax, slow down
catch one's eye*:VP	7	125	attract
catch someone off guard:VP	7	118	surprise, alert
catch someone red-handed*:VP	7	125	find direct evidence of guilt
catch up with**:PV	7	128	hit a limit & have a negative effect; get back to
catch**:VP	6	99	see, attend, reach
catch*:NP	1	12	drawback, desirable mate
catch-22*:NP	1	12	impossible situation
catch-22**:NP	8	146	impossible situation
CEO**:NP	3	44	chief executive officer
channel surf**:VP	5	88	flip through TV stations with remote control, SL
charge**:VP	8	145	make pay, fine
charmed life**:NP	8	140	privileged lifestyle
chase**:VP	6	105	follow, try to meet, pick up on, hit on, SL
cheap shot**:NP	8	135	joke at someone's expense, SL
cheat on**:PV	3	40	be unfaithful, dishonest
check out**:PV	1	7	get information, look at; leave a hotel
check someone out**:PV	7	126	look at, inspect
chew out:PV	8	123	scold, SL
chicken**:NP	2	27	wimp, gutless, scared person
chill out**:PV	6	94	calm down, lighten up, SL
chip in:PV	5	80	contribute, help
chip off the old block*:NP	5	87	take after, resemble
chip on one's shoulder*:NP	5	87	quick tempered person due to inferiority complex
chutzpa**:NP	8	134	courage, nerve (Yiddish), SL
circles**:NP	8	135	social group
clean up one's act*:VP	6	106	behave better, more appropriately
click:VP	4	58	get along well; come to understand, SL
clue*:NP	2	32	hint, evidence
clueless*:ADJP	2	32	ignorant, empty headed, SL
clumsy**:ADJP	5	76	awkward, uncoordinated, klutzy
cold feet*:NP	5	86	fearful of commitment
cold turkey:ADVP	5	78	give up something completely
come across*:PV	5	86	give an impression; discover
come off it*:VP	5	85	stop trying to pretend
come off*:PV	5	85	effect, impression, result
come off**:PV	7	126	effect, impression, result
come on to*:PV	5	86	make sexual advances, pick up, hit on, SL
come on*:PV	5	86	hurry up; try; stop joking
come out of the woodwork**:VP	R	159	keep appearing incessantly
come out smelling like a rose:VP	6	98	off the hook, give a good impression after controversy
come out with**:PV	8	144	produce

Expression	Chapter	Page	Meaning
dry**:ADJP	R	151	not exciting
dump**:VP	6	105	break up with someone in an insensitive way, SL
dweeb**:NP	8	138	super geek, SL
easy-going**:ADJP	3	41	mellow, relaxed, calm
egghead**:NP	8	137	smart person, SL
end of story**:NP	7	127	face the facts, reality
end up**:PV	6, 8	106, 146	result in
even out*:PV	2	32	make even, distribute equally
even steven*:ADJP	2	32	fair, equally divided, SL
even the score*:VP	2	32	get even, get back at, make fair
everything under the sun**:NP	1	2	the whole nine yards
face**:VP	7	128	accept
fad**:NP	1	8	trend
fair game*:NP	8	144	OK to attack
fair share**:NP	7	126	equal part
fair weather friend*:NP	1	13	your friend only if you're successful
fall apart**:PV	7	127	end, crumble
fall back on:PV	6	98	count on, have a back-up plan, protection
fall for something**:PV	6, 7	107, 124	buy into, believe something
fat chance**:NP	R	158	a shot in the dark, SL
fed up with**:PV	7	126	sick and tired of, have had enough
feed someone a line*:VP	7	124	deliberate flattery
feed someone's ego**:VP	2	28	flatter, give compliments, SL
feel like**:VP	2	33	in the mood for, want to
feel up to**:PV	2	33	have the energy and desire to do something
fierce**:ADJP	6	101	tough, aggressive, hardball
fight tooth and nail**:VP	R	159	aggressive, play hardball
fight tooth and nail**:VP	R	151	argue, defend vigorously
figurehead**:NP	7	118	symbol
figure out**:PV	1, 5	3, 88	solve, understand how
figure**:VP	7	126	assume, suppose
fill out**:PV	4	60	complete
find out**:PV	3, 7	40, 126	discover, learn
fish, meat person**:NP	6	94	what a person prefers to eat
five-star**:ADJP	5	84	the very best rating
flake out*:PV	2	32	be unreliable, SL
flake, a:NP	2	23	unreliable person; odd, SL
flaky*:ADJP	2	32	unreliable, odd, eccentric, SL
flick**:NP	6	106	movie, film, SL
flip (out):VP	4	62	become excited; crazy; angry, SL
flip off*:PV	4	69	a vulgar gesture using one's finger, SL
flip someone out**:PV	R	146	freak someone out, SL
flip your lid*:VP	4	69	lose control of one's temper or composure, SL
flip*:VP	4	69	toss to decide
flip-flop*:ADVP	4	69	opposite of what's expected, go back and forth
flippy**:ADJP	R	146	strange, bizarre, SL
flop**:NP	R	146	a failure, SL
folks**:NP	3	53	parents; relatives; people
food for thought:NP	2	20	something worth reflection
fool yourself**:VP	4	70	lie to oneself
for real**:ADVP	1	14	genuine, true, SL
freak (out)**:VP	4	62	go crazy, lose control, SL
freak**:NP	8	138	strange, weird, eccentric person, SL
freaky**:ADJP	8	137	bizarre, unexplainable

Expression	Chapter	Page	Meaning
go for a spin*:VP	5	88	go for a leisurely drive
go for**:VP	1, 6	14, 95	attempt, try. give it a shot, SL
go in circles**:VP	5	79	spin one's wheels, make no progress
go out of one's way**:VP	2	27	bend over backwards
go out on:PV	3	40	stop functioning; cheat on
go out**:PV	7	127	socialize in public places
go through with**:PV	6	107	complete, finish, do something challenging
go through**:PV	4	65	sort, finish
go through**:PV	7	128	experience a challenging time
go through**:PV	8	145	finish, use up
go too far**:VP	8	135	exceed the limit
golden opportunity**:NP	1	15	once in a lifetime chance
good old boys**:NP	7	127	group of male friends
goof off**:PV	7	126	play around
gossip**:NP	6	100	rumors, talk too much behind peoples' backs
Grammy**:NP	8	144	music award
grand slam**:NP	7	119	homerun, great
great new turn**:NP	7	127	a positive change
grin and bear it:CL	5	80	endure, put up with, tolerate
gripe:VP	7	118	complain, moan
grouchy**:ADJP	7	117	cranky, grumpy
grow on someone:PV	2	25	start to like, become fond of over time
grow up**:PV	7	115	be raised, become an adult
grumpy**:ADJP	7	115	cranky, grouchy
gut*:NP	1	13	intuition; big belly
gutless*:ADJP	1	13	no courage, wimpy
guts:NP	1	4	courage; nerve
gutsy*:ADJP	1	13	nervy, audacious, courageous, brazen
gutsy**:ADJP	8	133	nervy, audacious, courageous, brazen
guy/girl thing**:NP	7	127	stereotypic gender behavior, SL
hammered**:ADJP	8	146	be very drunk, SL
handle**:VP	7	128	manage, deal with, control
hang out**:PV	6	107	spend time with, socialize
hard core**:ADJP	7	127	extreme
hard pressed**:ADJP	6	98	challenged to do something
hassle:NP	4	60	inconvenience, bother, disagree
have it made**:VP	8	136	be guaranteed success
have nerve*:VP	8	143	audacious, obnoxious
have one's hands full**:VP	8	146	be too busy
have one's heart set on**:VP	7	127	strongly desire something
have what it takes:VP	2	20	possess necessary qualities
head for**:PV	8	146	go to a destination
held up*:ADJP	4	68	stuck, can't move
help someone out**:PV	6	100	assist
hip**:ADJP	8	138	savvy, up-to-date, informed, SL
hit a nerve*:VP	8	143	disturb
hit it big*:VP	4	68	make a lot of money
hit it off:PV	4	60	click, get along well
hit it*:CL	4	68	start; leave, SL
hit on*:PV	4	68	pick up, make sexual advances, SL
hit on**:PV	7	126	pick up, make sexual advances, SL
hit rock bottom*:VP	4	67	at the lowest point, very depressed, sad
hit someone up for something*:VP	4	68	ask something to lend or give something
hit the bars**:VP	7	118	go drinking at many places

Expression	Chapter	Page	Meaning
know something inside out**:VP	4	63	understand completely
know the ropes:VP	5	76	understand everything about how a place functions
know-how**:NP	4	62	savvy, understand
laid off**:ADJP	4	70	lose one's job due to lack of business
lame:ADJP	8	135	inconsiderate, inadequate, stupid, SL
land something**:VP	7	127	get, receive, earn, work for
lay something on the line*:VP	7	127	be very direct, straight
leads*:NP	2	32	tips, places to start, guide
learn one's lesson**:VP	8	145	learn through experience
learn the hard way*:VP	4	105	learn through life experience
learn the hard way**:VP	6	180	learn through life experience
left-wing**:ADJP	5	86	very liberal
let one's guard down*:VP	7	127	become vulnerable, open up
let something slide**:VP	7	127	be lenient, soft
lift**:NP	5	88	a ride
lighten one's load**:VP	5	180	relax, take pressure off, SL
lighten up:PV	6	98	calm down, relax, take the pressure off, SL
line of work**:NP	6	105	type of profession
line*:NP	7	124	type of work
lips are sealed**:P	7	126	will keep a secret
loaded**:ADJP	1,8	3, 145	have all the extra accessories; be rich, SL
look what the cat dragged in**:CL	2	24	finally back
loopy**:ADJP	8	141	crazy, off the wall, SL
lose it**:VP	8	145	go crazy, out of control, SL
lotto**:NP	6	94	lottery
lousy**:ADJP	8	174	bad, not good, crummy, SL
make a comeback:NP	8	132	become successful again, witty remark
make a long story short**:VP	1	7	in a nutshell
make ends meet:VP	8	135	live within one's means
make it**:VP	2	26	achieve success
make one's head spin*:VP	5	86	feel dizzy, confused
make out*:PV	1	13	able to read, hear; kiss
make out:PV	1	6	do well, succeed
man**:ADVP	1	7	what?! wow!, SL
material girl**NP	8	145	yuppie, gold digger, SL
max out:PV	4	60	hit, reach the limit, SL
mega-giant**:NP	2	29	extremely large, powerful and important, SL
mess with**:VP	2	24	cause trouble, SL
messed up**:ADJP	7	127	wrong, twisted, SL
mind in the gutter*:NP	7	127	think vulgar thoughts
miss one's calling*:VP	6	105	should be in a different line of work that's more fitting
miss the boat**:VP	4	61	be off base, not understand, lose an opportunity
moan**:VP	7	118	gripe, complain, SL
mouth off**:VP	1	10	speak rudely
move in on*:PV	8	145	take over to gain control
move on:PV	8	135	carry on by changing one's behavior, SL
Mr. Right*:NP	5	86	perfect man, best mate
munch**:VP	4	70	eat, snack, SL
Murphy's Law**:NP	R	150	pessimistic realism
muster up**:PV	7	126	find strength, courage
narrow-minded*:ADJP	5	180	small town mentality, not open, unsophisticated
neck*:VP	1	13	kiss, SL
nerves of steel*:NP	8	143	tough, calm under pressure

Expression	Chapter	Page	Meaning
pitch in**:PV	6	107	chip in, help, contribute
play around**:PV	6	107	goof off, relax,
play around*:PV	6	105	cheat on
play catch-up*:VP	1	12	always be in a rush to finish
play doctor*:VP	6	105	pretend to be a doctor
play dumb*:VP	6	105	pretend to be ignorant
play games**:VP	6	108	not be honest with someone
play hard*:VP	6	105	have a lot of fun
play hardball:VP	6	96	aggressive, tough on negotiations, challenge, stubborn
play hard-to-get*:VP	6	105	act uninterested
play hooky*:VP	3	51	ditch school, not attend what you should
play it by ear:VP	3	40	do things as they happen, spontaneous
play it cool*:VP	3	50	be calm, controlled, SL
play it safe*:VP	3	50	don't take risks
play it straight*:VP	3	50	behave honestly, directly
play nurse**:VP	6	106	pretend to be a nurse
play patient**:VP	6	106	pretend to be a patient
play the game*:VP	6	105	follow the rules, red tape, go along
pointers**:NP	2	20	tips, hints, suggestions
porno**:NP	7	127	pornography, SL
possessive**:ADJP	7	127	insecure behavior
pot belly*:NP	1	13	a large, protruding stomach
potluck**:ADJP	5	81	contribute one's part
practical joke:NP	7	112	planned trick
practical joke*:NP	3	51	planned trick
prank**:NP	7	112	joke, trick
pretty penny**:NP	8	132	expensive
proceeds**:NP	8	144	money
promise the sun, moon, stars**:VP	6	107	the whole nine yards, everything
public eye**:NP	8	144	be in the news
pull a fast one*:VP	7	124	trick to gain advantage
pull one's leg*:VP	7	124	trick, joke, kid
pull oneself together*:PV	7	124	calm down, compose oneself
pull something off:PV	7	112	do the unexpected successfully, get away with
pull something off **:PV	2	27	do the unexpected successfully, get away with
pump iron**:VP	7	119	lift weights for muscle building, SL
pumped up:ADJP	7	115	excited, motivated, SL
punk**:NP	1	9	young street criminal, SL
push one's luck:VP	1	2	continued risk after success
push someone away**:PV	6	106	make reject
put off**:PV	7	116	delay, wait; displease
put on airs**:VP	5	181	arrogant, show off, boast
put one's money...one's mouth is**:VP	8	146	do what you say you're going to do
put one's spin on something*:VP	5	86	giving one's unsolicited opinion or point of view
put one's cards on the table**:VP	R	155	frank, up front
put something off**:PV	7	128	postpone, delay
put the moves on*:VP	8	143	make advances, pick up
put up with**:PV	5	81	tolerate, grin and bear it
quack**:NP	2	24	a charlatan, fake
quit**:VP	7	120	stop, give up

Expression	Chapter	Page	Meaning
sleep it off**:PV	8	146	sleep to lose effect of alcohol
slick:ADJP	8	132	smooth; clever, SL
slopes**:NP	3	51	sides of mountains as in ski slopes
snob**:ADJP	R	158	arrogant, stuck-up, feels superior
snooze:VP	4	60	sleep
snotty**:ADJP	6	99	obnoxious superior attitude, snobby
so far so good**:ADVP	4	58	everything up to the present is fine
sore loser**:NP	8	136	poor sport, doesn't like to lose, SL
sound advice**:NP	6	95	trustworthy advice
sources*:NP	2	32	tips, root of information
spaced out:ADJP	2	20	out of touch, fatigued, SL
spank**:VP	8	143	hit to punish
speak of the devil:ADVP	2	23	think/ about someone who then appears
spill your guts*:VP	1	13	confess your true feelings
spin doctor*:NP	5	86	someone who gives unsolicited opinions, SL
spin one's wheels:VP	5	78	work hard with little or no result
spin out*:PV	5	86	move in circles and lose control
spot**:VP	7	127	detect, observe, find
spunk**:NP	1	9	energy, guts, SL
squeeze in**:PV	8	143	find room for
stab in the back*:VP	8	143	deceive
stand someone up**:PV	6	107	not show up for a date
stand up for**:PV	6	107	defend, back up
stand up to someone**:PV	7	126	confront
stand-up**:ADJP	8	132	live performance
startle**:VP	7	118	surprise, scare, catch off guard
stay in touch**:VP	2	34	remain in contact via mail, phone, keep in touch
stay on top**:VP	8	138	keep up with, be in a favorable position
stick it out**:VP	5	89	tough it out, endure, grin and bear it, not give up
stick out like a sore thumb*:VP	5	87	very noticeable
stick to**:VP	7	127	adhere to, follow
stick up for*:PV	5	87	defend, back up
stick your neck out:VP	5	80	risk, go for it, get up the nerve
sticky*:ADJP	5	87	delicate, touchy,
stoked**:ADJP	1	7	jazzed, SL
straight away**:ADJP	R	158	immediately
straight:ADJP	1	2, 11	traditional; honest; SL
straight*:ADJP	1	12	not gay, no longer criminal, SL
straighten out**:PV	6	106	improve one's behavior
straighten up**:PV	6	107	clean up, make tidy; behave oneself
stunt**:NP	7	114	trick
sugary**:ADJP	7	124	too sweet, touchy-feely
suit one's fancy**:VP	8	136	one's tastes, likes
swear**:VP	1, 7	6, 115	promise; use offensive language
tacky:ADJP	4	58	in poor taste, inappropriate
tailgate party**:NP	3	56	picnic in parking lot before sports event
tailgate:VP	3	43	drive too closely behind another motorist
take a long hard look**:VP	5	88	face something difficult in an honest way
take a stand**:VP	6	108	support a cause
take advantage of**:VP	1	3	treat unfairly, expect
take by surprise**:VP	7	112	catch unaware
take it with a grain of salt**:CL	7	118	no big deal, don't make it important
take it*:VP	2	32	endure the pressure
take off**:PV	2, 7	20, 126	be absent, leave; become successful

Expression	Chapter	Page	Meaning
top-notch**:ADJP	7	119	the best quality
touch base*:VP	4	68	check in on, contact
touch on*:PV	7	123	mention
touch up*:PV	7	123	fix, make perfect
touchy-feely*:ADJP	7	123	overly concerned with feelings
touchy:ADJP	7	112	sensitive, sticky
tough act to follow:NP	6	98	difficult to replace, follow
tough to swallow**:VP	8	136	difficult to accept, SL
tough**:ADJP	1, 2, 7	3, 34, 116	hard; difficult, challenging; unfortunate, SL
toughen up**:PV	7	127	become strong, hardened
turn bright red**:VP	7	126	become embarrassed
turn in **:PV	1	2	submit
turn out**:PV	1	10	become, result in
twist my arm:VP	4	58	convince to do in a joking way
two-timer**:NP	1	5	disloyal partner
Uncle Sam**:NP	7	128	symbol of the U.S. government
under one's belt*:ADVP	8	144	have some experience
under the gun**:ADVP	6	98	under pressure
under the table**:ADVP	7	128	receive money without paying taxes
up for*ADJP	2	33	feel like, in the mood for
up front*:ADJP	2	33	direct, straight, honest
up to no good**:ADVP	7	124	do something bad or illegal
up to*:ADJP	2	33	what's been happening
up*:ADJP	2	33	positive, in a good mood
update**:NP	4	70	the most recent information, status
uptight:ADJP	3	40	nervous, tense, SL
vicious circle**:NP	6	108	inescapable cycle, catch-22
wacky:ADJP	8	137	crazy, nuts, bizarre, SL
wannabe**:NP	2	21	someone who wants to be what they aren't, SL
wasted**:ADJP	8	146	be very drunk, SL
way to go**:CL	5	89	great, right on, SL
weird**:ADJP	3	43	bizarre, strange, off the wall, funny, SL
what you don't know can hurt you**:CL	7	127	warning to stay informed
what you see is what you get**:CL	4	59	the bottom line, the way it is, no change
what's up**:CL	2	33	what is happening
what's the deal*:CL	2	33	what's the situation what's happening
whine**:VP	7	119	complain in an irritating manner, SL
wimp, a:NP	2	25	a chicken, someone with no guts, SL
wine and dine:VP	1	4	treat to a nice meal; schmooze
wiped out:PV	7	118	destroy; eliminate; exhaust, SL
wisecrack:NP	3	43	joke, sarcastic remark, SL
wiseguy*:NP	3	51	practical joker, prankster, SL
wishy-washy**:ADJP	3	46	indecisive, SL
work out**:PV	5	86	result in, turn out
work**:VP	8	138	achieve, function, happen
workaholic:NP	6	97	someone who works too much
wouldn't touch with a 10-foot pole*:VP	7	124	stay away from completely
write home about**:VP	6	95	event worth remembering
write the book on**:VP	4	63	be an authority on a subject
yuppie:NP	1	6	materialistic young professional
zany**:ADJP	8	137	crazy, wacky, nuts, SL